WINNING THE HOMEWORK WAR

Kathleen M. Anesko, Ph.D.
and
Fredric M. Levine, Ph.D.

ARCO
New York

Lovingly dedicated to
Lawrence and Betty Anesko
who facilitated good homework habits,
and to Marilyn, Sam, and Max Levine
so that homework wars do not occur.

 ARCO

Simon & Schuster, Inc.
15 Columbus Circle
New York, NY 10023

DISTRIBUTED BY PRENTICE HALL TRADE SALES

Manufactured in the United States of America

3 4 5 6 7 8 9 10

Library of Congress Cataloging-in-Publication Data

Anesko, Kathleen M.
  Winning the homework war.

  Bibliography: p.
  Includes index.
  1. Homework. 2. Education–Parent participation.
I. Levine, Fredric M. II. Title.
LB1048.A54 1987   371.3′028′12   87-7334
ISBN 0-13-960956-3

Contents

1: Introduction   1

Homework Research
Parents' Involvement in Homework
Common Homework Problems
Developing Good Homework Habits

2: Before Beginning   13

Visual Problems
Auditory Problems
Mismatch of Academic Abilities and
    Expected School Performance
Learning Disabilities
Attention Problems

3: The Development of Habits   27

Importance of Repetition
Principles of Association
Principles of Reinforcement and
    Punishment
Individual Definition of Reinforcement

Contents

Increasing the Effectiveness of
    Reinforcement
Dangers of Punishment When Applied
    to Homework
Shaping
Intermittent Reinforcement
Review of Principles

4: Pinpointing Your Child's
   Specific Homework Problems   46

The Homework Problem Checklist
The Most Common Homework Problems
Talking to the Teacher
Analyzing the Home Situation
Attacking the Problem
Describing and Observing the Problem

5: Getting Homework Home   68

Solutions to Getting Homework Home
Daily Homework Record

6: Where and When to Do Homework   86

Designing a Study Area
Basic Study Rules
Some Problem Types

7: How to Do Homework   108

Defusing the "Homework War"
Off to a Good Start
Setting Realistic Homework Goals
Parental Attention, Approval, and
    Encouragement

Contents

Natural Incentives
Ignoring
Parents as Homework Consultants
Self-Instruction Training

8: Projects, Papers, and Taking Tests
(Tips for the Older Student)   144

Projects and Papers
Defining Your Goal
Figuring Out What Information is
    Needed and Available
Developing an Outline
Identifying People as Resources
Preparing For and Taking Tests
Preparing For the Exam
Test Taking Tips

9: Conclusion   172

Association and Reinforcement
Homework Rules
Case Histories: Mario and Joe
Illustration of Warfare in the Family
Charting Progress
When More Help is Needed
Final Word

Homework Program Evaluation   191

Research Findings of the Homework Clinic
Homework Program Case Studies

Contents

Bibliography and Other Recommended
Reading for Parents   207

Index   211

Acknowledgement

The authors appreciate Marilyn Levine's very helpful comments, and the Three Village, Smithtown, Hauppauge, Middle Country, and Port Jefferson school districts for their cooperation in the homework research.

We are most indebted to the parents and children who were involved in the homework program for their efforts in helping us evaluate it.

1

Introduction

Does this sound familiar?

"Billy, do your homework!" yells Billy's mother for the third time. Billy says he will as he continues to watch television. "Listen, I'm tired of telling you to do your homework. Get upstairs before I get your father to drag you up!!" Billy says he'll do his homework when the commercial starts. . . .

Or, how about this?

"Mom, I forgot my homework. I left it (a) on the bus, (b) in my locker, (c) in my desk, (d) _____ _____ [enter your child's creative response here.]"

Perhaps this conversation is more common in your home:

"What do you mean you don't understand the assignment? Where were you when the teacher explained it? In Timbuktu?"

These scenes are typical of just about every household with school-aged children. Homework almost never tops a child's list of "favorite things to do," and parents often have to prod, push, coax, beg, or threaten in order to get the work underway. At times, parents may actually be at war with their kids over homework. As psychologists who have worked with frazzled families and done research on homework, we are aware how intense homework wars can become. They can often dominate family life in an ugly and destructive way.

Homework Research

Are parental concerns about homework and how it's done justified? Current research would suggest they are. About 75 percent of children referred to psychological clinics perform poorly at school. School achievement is related to the emotional adjustment of both children and adults. Children who do poorly in school tend to be less liked by classmates, they are labeled as behavior problems by teachers, and they have low self-esteem.

Over the last few years the American public has voiced growing concern about the quality of education available to its children. The publication of *A Nation at Risk*, written by the National Commission on Excellence in Education (1983), generated a call for educational reform as it pointed out that the achievement of American students compared unfavorably with that of students in other countries such as Japan and most of those in Europe. In one of its major findings, the report cited evidence that the amount of homework assigned to American high-school seniors had decreased, with two-thirds of the students polled reporting that they did less than one hour of homework each night. The Commission recommended substantial increases in the amount of assigned homework, a recommendation supported by several studies that found that homework and the time spent on its completion directly affect grades and achievement-test scores. For example, a survey of over twenty thousand high-school seniors found that the amount of time spent on homework was second only to intellectual ability in predicting school grades.

Despite these favorable findings, much debate over the merits and shortcomings of homework has taken place during the past twenty years. Children, even in studies dating back to the 1930s, usually report disliking homework. On the one hand, parents and educators alike have argued that many homework assignments are "busy work" tasks that often go unreviewed by instructors and fail to take into account individual learning differences among students. Others counter that completion of homework strengthens academic skills taught in the classroom, develops self-discipline, and fosters the ability to work independently.

In spite of this controversy, public sentiment, as measured by recent Census Bureau findings (1983) and opinion-poll surveys (Gallup, 1984; 1985), not only favors the continued practice of assigning homework but also supports increasing the amount of homework given to children of all ages. The majority of parents surveyed in one poll said that their elementary school-aged children were not required to work hard enough (Gallup, 1984), while 40 percent of parents in another study favored increased homework for their grade-school children (Gallup, 1985). As more and more school districts adopt policies requiring nightly homework assignments, children and parents alike are facing greater demands to see that the work is completed. With students not yet in high school, homework is rarely a solitary activity. According to one of the most recent Gallup polls on public schools, a large majority of parents help their youngsters with homework.

How does parental involvement in homework affect family life? In one study, educators from Columbia's Teachers' College observed twelve blue-collar households and found that in each case families reshaped their activities around homework. For example, at least one parent in each family supervised the homework to some degree, his or her involvement ranging from reminders to start working, to checking work for mistakes and direct tutoring. These educators concluded that these practices were representative of homework's effects on the lives of most families with school-aged children.

Parents' Involvement in Homework

The work of researchers in Germany (Plessen and Bommert, 1978) and the U.S. (Anesko, Shoiock, Ramirez, and Levine, in press) suggests that most parents do report the existence of homework-related problems. These parents identified common difficulties—delays in completing homework, poor execution of the work and resistance to parental correction, and trouble establishing a good study routine—that may may contribute to homework-related tension between parent and child. In other words, readers take heart: you're not alone!

Although many studies have reported programs that teach parents how to modify their own children's behavior problems and teach teachers how to manage behavior in the classroom, few have reported how parents can be taught to help their children directly with school homework. This book integrates the findings from these studies with the results of a two-year project we conducted that evaluated the effectiveness of a manual written for parents of early-grade-school children that outlined strategies for handling common homework problems. The purpose of this book is to present a program, adapted from these studies, that parents can follow to help their youngsters complete assignments with a minimum of headaches, while promoting good study habits that, in turn, can positively affect academic performance. The program is based on simple, well-established principles of psychology and has succeeded in reducing homework problems both in research studies and when used by therapists in their work with families. If you follow the program guidelines consistently, you and your child will probably notice an improvement in homework skills and in four to six weeks see a noticeable decrease in family tension related to homework completion. Thirty-five families in one study conducted by us reported significant drops in homework-related problems after one month, and most continued to report minimal homework difficulties more than a year after their active use of the program had ended. Those parents and children who experienced the greatest improvement in their homework interactions had integrated program strategies into their household's daily homework routine, and we encourage you to do the same.

If you are still skeptical about your ability to change your current homework struggle, parents *can* make a difference when it comes to influencing their children's attitudes toward school and their interest in learning. According to a recent report published by the University of Illinois, as much as one-half the difference in student grades and test scores can be attributed to parent participation in school-related activities at home. And you don't need to be a college-educated or well- to-do parent in order to be effective, either. What does seem to be essential, according to this research, is how well you communicate to your youngster that schooling is valued by the family and that you are confident your child can, and will, succeed in the classroom. We believe this process is best started during the child's early years in school; that is why much of the program suggestions and strategies focus on the development of good homework/study habits at the time when home assignments are first given, generally when the child is in first or second grade. That is not to say that older

For Better or For Worse. © 1984 Universal Press Syndicate. Reprinted with permission. All rights reserved.

children cannot be taught to study well, only that this process is usually harder, since these boys and girls have several years of bad or ineffective study skills to unlearn. Their families, too, have probably participated in more arguments and fights about schoolwork, and will need more practice in approaching homework interactions with a positive, problem-solving (not problem-finding) outlook before homework time becomes peaceful for all.

Common Homework Problems

Let's examine some of the more common homework hassles that face families today and how they negatively affect both parents and children. Which ones sound familiar? See if you can figure out what the child and the parent(s) may be doing that is contributing to the problems these families are experiencing.

We have seen many families for whom getting youngsters to complete homework is a nightmare. Sixteen-year-old Sam never says that he doesn't want to do homework. He always says, "Yeah, Mom, in just a minute. As soon as this TV program is over." When the program is over, Sam still doesn't say "no"; he says, "Yeah, Mom, just as soon as *this* program is over." We all know that there are always programs on television. After several "Sure, Moms," Mom has had it. She loses control and tells Sam that if he doesn't do his homework, he will not be allowed to leave the house until he is married and has three children. He will be forbidden to watch television, and if he objects, he will be put on a bread-and-water diet. Naturally, these threats are not carried out and Sam goes back to saying, "Yeah, Mom, just as soon as this program is over."

On the other hand, twelve-year-old Susan simply says that she doesn't have homework and that she did it in school. Although her mother can't quite understand how Susan doesn't have homework when many of her classmates do, she accepts Susan's claim. After all, it is not impossible that Susan was able to finish her homework in school. However, when report-card time comes, guess what? Susan's teacher notes that Susan has not been handing in assignments. Both parents are furious and march in to see the teacher to find out how serious the problem is. The teacher tells them that Susan has turned in less than half of the required work. Susan is sent to her room to do homework every evening after supper from 7:00 to 9:30, whether she has homework or not. Sometimes Susan sits in her room and does nothing. She says she has no homework.

Then, of course, there is nine-year-old Joseph, who loves to play with his friends. He never forgets an invitation to play, even though his social schedule is complicated. Why, then, does he always lose his homework assignments? When he remembers, he does his homework without complaint. But often the night is spent trying to call a classmate who has the assignment. His parents have threatened him with not being allowed to play with his friends, even though they know that he loves being with them and that friends are good for him. Why can't he just remember to bring home his assignments?

We cannot forget easygoing Scott. Scott remembers to bring home his assignments. Scott always begins homework with only slight grumbling and then stays at his desk . . . and stays at his desk . . . and stays at his desk. He daydreams, doodles, and diddles. Very little homework gets done. And this little bit of homework takes a great deal of time to do. But Scott stays at his desk.

The parents in all of these cases reported to us that they had tried everything. They told us that they have punished the child with no television, grounding, and more. They have also rewarded the child with things like a bicycle when homework was finished every day for a month. And almost all parents have yelled and threatened and cajoled. Sadly, these parents tell us that their youngsters still have not developed good, solid homework routines.

Developing Good Homework Habits

The development of homework habits is of vital importance to youngsters. Most directly affected by poor homework habits is school performance, as grades are substantially lowered. The development of any skill requires practice. Doing homework provides the drill that is necessary for the material presented in school to be fully learned. Without that drill, many children find that they really did not understand the material as well as they thought they did. Unfortunately, this realization often occurs only after tests are returned with low marks.

When children are able to do homework as a regular routine and can show pride in their achievements, their grades improve. Not only do they feel better about themselves but more doors are opened to those who perform well. They are able to get into college more easily, and often to get better jobs. The development of homework habits also helps in the development of work habits. After all, schoolwork is to the child what paid work is to the adult. Because schoolwork also involves homework—the bringing home of work—it means that the youngster is under steady pressure. When children learn to handle the pressure of this job, they are also developing sound work habits. The development of work habits is the single most important factor in determining career success. Although there are exceptions, generally those people who are able to work hard are those who do better vocationally.

Having poor homework habits can also affect the child socially. We have seen many children who have been on the "bad side" of teachers because they do not complete homework. Teachers sometimes label these children "lazy" or "defiant," and these labels influence how the teachers relate to the youngsters. Having a teacher angry at a child often leads the child to become less motivated in school or simply more negative. When the child does poorly in school, the child often makes friends with those of like behavior. These children tend to support each other in doing poorly in school, and many develop antischool attitudes.

Not doing homework almost always puts a strain on family relationships. A large percentage of youngsters who came into the community outpatient clinic at the State University of New York at Stony Brook, where we worked, were referred because of academic problems, including homework difficulties. Very often parents were furious at the child, and that fury interfered with other areas of family life. We could hear the angry tone parents used with the children, and noted how, when homework was left undone, this anger prevented these families from enjoying the time they spent together.

The children, likewise, were angry with their parents. They had heard a disproportionate amount of criticism, and were rarely praised. To them, their parents were often overly controlling and overly hostile. These angry youngsters learned effectively to tune out their parents' critical remarks and, at times, deliberately did poorly to retaliate against their folks.

We were aware that most of the parents were well meaning in their attempts to prompt their children to complete homework. They did not enjoy getting angry with their sons and daughters, but felt helpless to bring about any positive changes in the family's homework "drama." We are quick to acknowledge how difficult it can be to be a parent. The job requires firmness and much patience. Parents have both an immediate responsibility to the child and a responsibility to the adult that the child will become. All too often the youngster is unable to see that the behavior of today can have a deep influence on adulthood. The parents must act as this bridge in time. It is difficult for a parent to be patient with a youngster who resists doing things for his or her own good, particularly when the parent is tired after a day of work at home or at the office. Using the principles described throughout this book will at first lead to more work for parents in tackling homework assignments. However, with continued practice, these principles lead to fewer conflicts between parents and children and to more cooperative attitudes toward schoolwork. The next chapter provides an overview of physical and learning problems that can contribute to homework difficulties, such as poor vision and specific learning disabilities. Chapter 3 outlines the two major principles of behavior, classical and operant learning, that form the foundation for the homework program detailed in chapters 4 through 9.

2

Before Beginning

Youngsters resist doing homework for many reasons, usually because they have not developed helpful homework habits. However, there are times when a number of other factors can make school more difficult for your child. We cannot assume that the task of doing homework is identical for all children. Schoolwork and homework are rarely individualized; rather, the work is generally designed for the child of average classroom ability. As a result, the same homework assignment may be very easy for some children, hard for others, and impossible for the rest. It is important to know your child's abilities in order to determine whether the homework and schoolwork he or she receives are at an appropriate level.

While the vast majority of youngsters we've seen have suffered from study-habit deficiencies, others have had physical problems or learning disabilities that interfered with homework performance. These problems had to be addressed first in order to help the child. The strategies for developing the good study skills outlined in this book could then be taught, but typically took longer before having a positive effect. In either case, a thorough assessment of the problems experienced by each child in relation to schoolwork is essential for remediation. Otherwise, parental expectations are often inapporpriately high and therefore impossible for the child to meet, so that conflict and tension occur within the family. Some common physical problems follow.

Visual Problems

Some children find doing schoolwork difficult and unpleasant because they have trouble seeing the work clearly and accurately. Parents should be alert to the warning signs, listed below, that are often indications of a variety of vision problems.

If the child has problems with **visual acuity**—the ability to focus clearly when looking at objects—reading and copying board-work will be more difficult. These children are typically referred to as being nearsighted, far-sighted, or as having an astigmatism. They may hold written material either unusually close to their faces or about an arm's length away when reading. Sometimes they will squint. They frequently make errors when copying from the board. Do not assume that the youngster will know that he or she cannot see well. One such thirteen-year-old was asked why he didn't report having difficulty seeing. He answered that he did not know there was any other way of seeing than the out-of-focus way in which the world appeared to him. His vision was the only standard for sight that he knew. If there is reason to believe that the child has an acuity problem, he or she should have his or her eyes examined by an optometrist or opthalmologist. Some children show marked improvement in their schoolwork after they have had corrective glasses prescribed.

There are also more subtle visual problems not specifically related to visual acuity that can be overlooked. For example, some children have difficulty with **visual convergence**, or the ability to coordinate and blend the images from each eye when looking at a nearby object. Children with this problem will see double when dealing with close material like reading or desk work. Sometimes simply asking the child whether he or she sees one image or two will pinpoint such difficulties. Other things to look for include a child who closes or covers one eye when reading or a child who constantly tilts his or her head to one side when reading or writing.

Other children have problems with **visual accommodation** and may have difficulty shifting the focus of their eyes from objects close to them to those farther away, and vice-versa. These children may also have trouble sustaining clear vision when looking at objects close to them for long periods of time (e.g., while reading or studying). It's not uncommon for these children to sit far from objects or people with whom they want to interact. They find it difficult to move their eyes back and forth from the blackboard to the book or paper because each time they shift their focus it becomes difficult to see clearly. As a result, their eyes tire easily and may become reddened and watery when the children are reading or writing. A child may complain that the print blurs after reading for a short time and that his or her eyes feel uncomfortable. We worked very hard with one such case, a boy of nine, and saw little improvement in his homework. We then noticed that he consistently moved his seat as far from us as he could. At the same time, we knew that he liked us and that we had a positive relationship. We referred him to an optometrist who specialized in the assessment and treatment of perceptual problems. The boy did considerably better after perceptual training helped him to accommodate more effectively; that is, to shift his visual focus smoothly from nearby to faraway objects.

Problems with **ocular coordination** occur when the child cannot accurately aim and control the movement of his or her eyes. Clues to these difficulties include a child who loses his or her place when reading unless a finger or ruler is used and who skips words and rereads lines.

These are just a few of the visual problems a child may develop that will interfere with learning and the satisfactory completion of schoolwork. If there are consistent indications of such problems, the youngster should be evaluated by an optometrist or opthalmologist trained to diagnose perceptual problems. A routine visual acuity test is neither sufficiently sensitive nor designed to assess the variety of skills needed to perceive and make sense of the visual information present in the classroom and in the world around us.

Auditory Problems

Once again, we have seen youngsters who experience enormous difficulty in school because they are unable to hear what is going on in the classroom. These children are often angry at their teachers for confusing them. If hearing difficulties aren't recognized, the teacher and the parent often tell the child to "pay attention," become angry and accuse the child of being lazy. Hearing problems may be indicated if the youngster consistently plays the television or radio at a loud volume or if the parent automatically raises his or her voice when speaking to the child. Other signs to which parents should be alert include the youngster who frequently gives inappropriate answers or often says "What?" or "Huh?" to questions. Concern is especially warranted if the child does not respond to positive sounds such as the bell of the neighborhood ice cream truck, as was the case with one child we saw. Children whose hearing is better on one side tend to favor that side by turning their heads toward the speaker and/or by placing themselves so that the better ear is closer to the speaker. The mildly to moderately hard-of-hearing child's comprehension of speech may drop if the speaker's voice becomes louder or softer or if the speaker turns away from the child while talking (e.g., a teacher turning to write on the blackboard).

Generally, these signs are more significant during the child's earlier years. Adolescents seem to feel cheated when the radio or television is not rocking the building. Teenagers also seem to attend less to parents than do younger children. If the adolescent appears to hear his or her friends easily but does not respond to the request of parents, a hearing loss can generally be ruled out. Otherwise, the youngster should undergo an audiological evaluation. The school performance of many of these children improves dramatically after a hearing loss is recognized. Often the hearing loss can be compensated for with hearing aids, and sometimes it helps just to have the child sit closer to the teacher. However, unless the hearing problem is addressed and strategies for coping with it are provided for the student, we are placing a very difficult burden on that child.

Just as a routine vision test may not rule out visual perceptual problems, there are some youngsters with normal hearing who have auditory perceptual problems. These problems can occur separately or in combination, but their overall effect is to make it difficult for the child to perceive and understand spoken language. Children with **auditory discrimination** problems, for example, will have trouble distinguishing between sounds and may often confuse similar-sounding words (like moon-soon, cap-cat). **Auditory memory** problems may be suspected when your child has trouble following multiple directions or fails to remember a sentence or series of words. Likewise, **auditory sequencing** problems may be apparent if your child recalls a series of directions but does not carry them out in the order in which they were given. Or, he or she may be able to repeat a list of words or numbers, but changes the sequence in which they were first spoken.

We gave an I.Q. test to an eight-year-old boy. On those tests that involved visual information, he scored in the upper end of the superior range of intellectual functioning. However, on those subtests that required auditory memory, he scored at a very low level. At the same time, we noticed that he seemed unable to filter out auditory distractions. His performance during the I.Q. test was poor while the air conditioner was on and considerably better when it was turned off. Most of us are able to "filter out" background noises that are not too loud, such as air conditioners. Not so, however, with this very bright youngster, who was often confused by what he heard. He specifically misbehaved in school in order to be suspended. He preferred home tutoring, where he didn't have to face all the sounds that fill a classroom during lessons (children whispering, pages rustling, coughs, the hum of the fluorescent lights, and so on). In this case, it was difficult to design a school placement that was quiet, and this unfortunate child had significant difficulties functioning in school. Despite being very bright, he was placed in small, special-education classes with students of lower general ability. He still became distracted and frustrated by competing sounds, and was often extremely angry.

Although few children fit into these categories of visual and auditory problems, it is important that parents be informed of their existence. We must be alert to the fact that youngsters can do poorly in school because of specific disabilities. These disabilities are often subtle and at times difficult to identify. Even trained psychologists have missed them.

Mismatch of Academic Abilities and Expected School Performance

I.Q., or one's intelligence quotient, is the most-often-used measure of academic ability. Psychologists are aware that I.Q. is one of many measures of intelligence. Howard Gardner, a Harvard psychologist, has presented a theory describing seven different types of intelligence that are separate from each other. We all know, for example, people who have done very well academically but cannot figure out how to turn the lock on a door. Academic intelligence is related to how well one does in school. If there is a significant mismatch between the child's academic abilities and the demands of the classroom, there are often problems in school that also involve resistance to doing homework.

A typical I.Q. test is scored so that the average person earns an I.Q. of 100. By definition, half the population will score at or above 100 on these tests and half will score below 100. For youngsters with an I.Q. below 90, the usual school curriculum will be difficult. As the I.Q. score gets lower, the youngster generally has more academic problems in a regular class setting. These students may need either the special attention provided by tutoring in a resource room or outside of the school, or they may need a curriculum that is better-suited to their academic level. It is important that these youngsters be formally tested. If your child's scores on group tests of academic abilities such as the Iowa Test of Basic Skills or the California Achievement Test indicate areas of weakness, an individual psychological test should be conducted. The individual tests are more reliable than the group tests and often reveal the child's strengths as well as weaknesses. They provide information that is more helpful when planning individual placement for the child.

Students can be frustrated if they are placed in a classroom that requires more from them than they are able to produce. These youngsters are often angry and defiant. Unless the school curriculum is adjusted to their capacities, school can be punishing for them.

Similarly, most of us would be frustrated and tuned out if we were placed in an advanced course in theoretical physics. Every class would be perceived as a failure. Most of us would withdraw rather than face predictable failure. If the demands of school can be adjusted to match these children's abilities more closely, "expectation of" failure can be reduced, as can resistance to homework.

In some cases, children with very high I.Q.s (over 125) may become bored with the level of work required in school. Although we have heard of such cases much more frequently than seen them, some of these youngsters do better when given an enriched curriculum. Educators should be consulted about whether there should be additional assignments or an enriched program. Some of these children may benefit from being advanced in school. Once again, we recommend that individual psychological testing be done to make a recommendation.

Learning Disabilities

Only since the 1960s have educators, psychologists, physicians, and legislators paid much attention to the existence of learning disabilities and their impact on children's ability to benefit from regular classroom instruction. Although no definition has met with universal acceptance, a learning disability is generally thought to refer to a specific area of academic difficulty experienced by a youngster of average-to-above-average I.Q. Research over the past twenty years has revealed three major areas of disability that involve problems in reading, spelling, and arithmetic as well as various subtypes within each skill area. Not uncommonly, a child is found to have significant learning problems in more than one skill area (e.g., reading and spelling).

In the past, these children were probably told that they were stupid, lazy, or that they just didn't care about school. Now, professionals are beginning to discover differences in how these children perceive, process, and apply visual and/or auditory information in relation to other children. Children referred to as "dyslexic" make up the largest group of learning-disabled students. They experience difficulty in reading and spelling; commonly seen problems include letter reversals, letter omissions and/or substitutions, and trouble in sounding out words by breaking them into their component parts. Other children are called "dysgraphic" when their learning problems involve poor spelling ability. Often these children make **phonetic** spelling errors. That is, they will spell words the way they sound (e.g., "offen" for "often") and, therefore, have trouble with homonyms (e.g., rain, rein, reign; to, too, two) and irregular words (e.g., whistle, label). In extreme cases, some children may lack the sensory-motor coordination required for writing, but read and perform arithmetic with little difficulty. The last major area of specific learning disability is "dyscalculia," which involves problems in carrying out mathematical operations. These children may have trouble printing numbers, lining up rows and columns of numbers, adding, subtracting, or multiplying in the appropriate direction, or following the correct sequence of steps in order to solve math problems.

Joey was a bright twelve-year-old who could not recognize letters. He had a severe case of dyslexia, but was a superb athlete and won state-wide awards in sports such as basketball and football, that required visual skill. He simply could not read, despite an above-average I.Q. Reading problems ran in his family—his father and sister had identical problems. At age twelve, with special education, he started to recognize letters and began to read. His teacher made up large stacks of reading cards for him. For weeks this boy would go through these cards with a thrilling determination. By age thirteen, he had functional reading skills and was still improving rapidly. If his dyslexia had been overlooked, he would not have received special education, and may have developed a negative self-image—a feeling of being stupid. Youngsters such as Joey may need special visual training and special education.

If you suspect that your child may have a specific learning disability, the youngster should receive individual psychological testing by a professional with some background in learning disabilities. Some clinical and school psychologists are qualified, but the parent should verify the tester's experience. The child's school is often a good source for referrals.

Attention Problems

Many youngsters have all the required abilities to do well in school but have little ability to remain attentive. These children constantly seek a variety of activities to keep them busy. They seem never to sit still and often get into trouble because of their curiosity. They like finding out what makes things work, so they take everything apart! They jump from one activity to another, and rarely complete any. The principles in this book are especially useful for these children. Parents must realize that these children simply cannot sit still as long as the parent may want.

One eight-year-old girl had great difficulty maintaining attention in her classroom activities and homework. Although most children with attention problems also have difficulty sitting still, she just drifted off and daydreamed during school and homework time. After we tried several approaches, unsuccessfully, we worked out a program whereby she was to give herself points for paying attention in school for a set period of time—say, fifteen minutes. When she earned enough points, she won a toy—in this case, a Smurf. After several weeks of marking her points, she developed the habit of paying attention and did considerably better.

Although we used the approach with this youngster, we do not advocate giving rewards for school performance without the recommendation of a psychologist. There are times when that approach can backfire, prompting the child to work only for rewards.

In some severer cases, generally diagnosed as "hyperactivity" or "attention-deficit disorder," youngsters may be helped by one of several medications that increase attention span. Ritalin, Dexedrine, and Cylert are the most common medications used to treat children with attention-deficit disorders. The major effect of these drugs is to increase concentration and sustain attention; decreased impulsiveness and disruptiveness are also frequently seen.

In other cases, however, it is medication taken for

physical problems such as epilepsy that can cause attentional difficulties. Research shows that youngsters on Phenobarbital or Dilantin often experience drowsiness initially, while some become more restless and distractible. These same side effects are occasionally noticed in children taking medication such as Theophylline or DSCG (cromolyn sodium) to control bronchial attacks associated with asthma.

All of the youngsters in the groups mentioned earlier can benefit from developing better homework habits. However, they may need additional services such as tutoring or placement in a resource room to perform at an appropriate level in school. Thus, it is very important to speak with your family doctor if your child is placed on medication; getting information about possible side effects that could interfere with classroom learning is critical. Even if no adverse side effects are anticipated, parents should pay attention to their child's academic performance and classroom behavior after medication is started. If difficulties at school begin to appear, notify your doctor at once so that he or she can conduct a medication review.

It is important that parents have a reasonable set of expectations about their child's academic ability. If the child is expected to do more than he or she is able, there is a likelihood that the child will rebel, not only in school work, but in other social areas as well. Frequently, these youngsters feel frustrated and picked on. Imagine the frustration of a youngster trying very hard to do well in school but unable to do so. Compound that with critical parents and teachers and it is easy to see why these children "tune out."

They can also become angry and rebellious when they feel they are trying and failing. Frustration can generate powerful negative self-images.

We have frequently gone over the psychological test results of children with learning disabilities and pointed out to them both their strengths and areas of difficulty. We specifically tell these children that they are not stupid, but rather that they have a problem that makes some school work harder. The majority of these youngsters have thought of themselves as being "dumb" and are relieved to be able to understand the nature of their difficulty. They are also told that, because of their disability, they have to work harder in some areas than other children.

Once an assessment is completed and sensory, perceptual, and learning disabilities are determined or ruled out, you can begin the homework program. If a disability is recognized and addressed, many children will do better quite rapidly. Many, however, have developed resistance to homework and will benefit from the program in this book. Parents can now have more realistic expectations for their children with disabilities and can set more appropriate goals. The program we will present should still be helpful after a disability is recognized even if progress occurs at a somewhat slower rate.

3

Development of Habits

In the previous chapters we spent a good deal of time detailing ways of defining your child's homework habits. We will now explore some useful psychological principles that can help your child overcome some of the difficulties he or she is having with homework. These principles can be used to improve even homework habits that are already good.

The first set of principles concerns the development of habits. Many of the children we see with homework problems have poor homework habits. By that we mean that they and their parents have not developed ways of doing homework in a *consistent* manner. By not developing consistent habits, these youngsters and their parents are continually faced with having to make decisions: "Should I do homework after school or before dinner?"; "Should I do homework at the kitchen table or at my desk?"; "Should I do homework with the radio on or off?" None of these questions is very difficult, but by asking them, your young-ster is prevented from developing good homework habits. In fact, not having routines invites youngsters to search for distractions. Once habits are developed these questions are not asked, and the youngster need not have his or her mind cluttered with choices that should be automatic.

When children are very young and have few habits, even ordinary hygiene routines are major issues. Toilet training is a way of developing habits of when, where, and how. The forming of habits is usually resisted in the beginning. However, with repetition we no longer have to go through hoops and hurdles to get Johnny to brush his teeth. The better the development of habits, the fewer the chances of interference. If Johnny brushes his teeth after breakfast *every day*, Johnny will not have to decide whether he should do it before breakfast, after breakfast, before dinner, or after dinner. Johnny's mind is freed from one of the many small decisions that can interfere with functioning.

Habits can work for us in a powerful way by making necessary areas of our lives automatic. Most of us wake up at the same time every work morning by habit. We have developed the "waking habit" to the extent that we often wake just before the alarm goes off. We even have habits that work while we sleep. Most of us have a routine morning schedule in which we take care of our toilet needs and our dressing order. We do not say, "Should I put my socks on before my trousers or my trousers on before my socks?" It would be very inefficient to clutter our minds with such trivial decisions. We prepare in the morning by habits—habits that were developed by repeated routines. These routines simplify our lives so that we can direct attention to decisions more important than whether socks should be put on before trousers.

Importance of Repetition

Habits are developed through practice, which is the process of repeating trials over and over until routines become automatic. Practice makes tasks that seem impossible easy and even automatic. When we first learn to drive a shift car, we usually think it is impossible that the right hand can shift while the left foot presses the clutch, the left hand controls the steering wheel, and the right foot is controlling both the accelerator and the brake. Even writing about simple shifting is complicated. However, with practice we do not even think about the multiple tasks that are involved in shifting. We do it automatically.

Once homework habits are developed, they will help the youngster do homework without the unnecessary interferences that create mischief. If Johnny does homework every day after supper, then Johnny doesn't have to decide whether he has time to do his homework after his favorite T.V. program is finished. The habit of doing homework after supper leads him to do it automatically after supper. If Jane decides she wants to do her homework as soon as she comes home from school and then does it every day, she no longer clutters her mind about whether she should play with her friends first. The habit decides for Jane. The job of the parent is to help the youngster develop useful habits. This is done by the development of routines.

29

At the turn of the century, William James, a professor at Harvard and one of the founders of modern psychology, compared the development of habits to the folding of a newspaper. He said that the more we fold a newspaper, the more readily it takes a specific shape. If we do it enough, it will refold itself.

More important, James stated that we must use the powerful forces of habit in an educational sense. "The great thing, then, in all education is to make [habits] an ally instead of our enemy. . . . For this we must make automatic and habitual, as early as possible, as many useful actions as we can, and guard against the growing into ways that are likely to be disadvantageous to us, as we should guard against the plague. The more of the details of our daily life we can hand over to the effortless custody of automatism, the more our higher powers of mind will be set free for their own proper work. There is no more miserable human being than one in whom nothing is habitual but indecision, and for whom the lighting of every cigar, the drinking of every cup, the time of rising and going to bed every day and the beginning of every bit of work, are subjects of express volitional deliberation."

The first of Professor James's findings about habits was that, with practice, a ". . . habit simplifies the movements required to achieve a given result, makes them more accurate and diminishes fatigue" (p. 117, *Principles of Psychology*, 1890). Obviously, this is one of the goals of developing positive homework habits, to simplify the movements and to increase accuracy. In addition, the development of habits will, in the long run, make less effort required for the homework to be begun and completed.

James's next rule of habits was that they ". . . diminish the conscious attention with which our acts are performed" (p. 119). This is another goal in developing homework habits. The youngster does not have to think about, or clutter his or her mind with, the when, the where, and the hows of homework. It becomes automatic. All too often, the youngster has not developed a simple habit of writing assignments down on an assignment pad. If this habit is not developed, a great deal of work and grief often occur when the youngster tries to reconstruct a homework assignment. When Jimmy does not have the habit of writing down assignments, Jimmy must call friends, and wastes time on trivia. Writing assignments should be automatic and not require conscious attention.

Principles of Association

Another important scientist in the development of rules for the creation of habits was Ivan Pavlov. In 1928, Pavlov reported a finding that became the basis for "classical" or "Pavlovian conditioning." He was interested in the salivation process in dogs. He connected the dogs' salivation ducts to tubes in order to measure the amount of saliva produced. In one experiment, he struck a tuning fork prior to feeding the dogs. At first the dogs, as expected, salivated after food was presented and did not salivate when the tuning fork was struck. However, after repeated trials, the dogs started to salivate when the tuning fork was sounded, without feeding. Pavlov called these salivations "psychic" secretions because they were not biological, but the result of training. The dogs associated the sound of the tuning fork with the food. Through this kind of conditioning, the tuning fork alone, merely because of its *association* with food, was enough to trigger the biological response—salivation.

Types of behaviors develop by association. Just as the food became associated with the tuning fork, we have learned that a red light is associated with stopping a car. It takes repeated practice for us to associate a red light with stopping. When soldiers are first in the army, they often have difficulty doing a "right face" on command. However, after hearing the command associated with the movements necessary to do a "right face," the soldiers can do it automatically.

These examples are used to show how we can associate a specific response with a specific stimulus event. Soldiers, without any conscious thought, will respond to the specific stimulus of "right face" with the correct turning maneuver. Just as the sound of the tuning fork automatically led to salivation in dogs, we associate certain specific stimulus events with specific responses.

Stimulus Control

A major Pavlovian technique used for the development of habits in specific situations is called a stimulus control procedure. Pavlov discovered that inanimate stimuli can develop the power to control our responses. A stimulus-control procedure is the development of a habit by associating a specific place with a specific response. The place, or stimulus, develops the power to control the response through repeated experiences. For example, overweight people often develop "bad" habits by eating while watching television or reading. Through association, they then become hungry whenever they watch television or read. Their eating response becomes controlled by the presence of the television. One weight-control procedure that has been successfully used requires the person who is attempting to lose weight to eat only at a specific place at the table. By repeatedly eating only at a specific place at the table and not eating while watching television or reading, the person soon only experiences the urge to eat when at the table.

Implications for Homework

Most of you have already seen the implications of the two principles—association and stimulus control—we have presented for the development of homework habits. Our challenge will be to change either the lack of habits, or the bad habits that have developed around the issue of homework. Let us look at which of your youngster's homework habits need work. Does Danny bring his assignments home every day? Does Karin do her homework at the same time every day? Does Carl do homework in the same place every day? Do you, as a parent, have a fixed schedule so that you can be available to help Brian develop homework habits?

It should be clear by now that once behaviors and habits are understood, we become less angry at our youngsters for not doing well. Frequently the youngster is none of the things we, as caring and frustrated parents, may think and say when we are angry—lazy, stupid, worthless, and more—but, rather, is a victim of not having habits that help him or her become successful. Our job is to help our youngster eliminate destructive habits and develop useful habits.

We should look at the two principles of repetition and association and through them observe the effect of current homework practices. Is homework done in a consistent manner, or is it frequently done irregularly? If there is little consistency, then there is little opportunity for positive habits to develop. Is homework associated with a specific location and time? Once again, if not, then positive homework habits are being inhibited.

Much of our program is based on James's theory of the development of habits—that of repeated practice—and Pavlov's theory of the development of associations through classical conditioning. We will give specific recommendations on how these principles can help your child develop better homework habits.

Principles of Reinforcement and Punishment

We develop habits through routines of repeated practice and through association with specific situations. We also develop habits that have proven useful to us: these habits have been reinforced. Reinforcement is the process by which behaviors are increased as a result of positive consequences *to the individual*. Punishment, on the other hand, is an opposite process by which behavior decreases when followed by negative consequences *to the individual*. These simple principles are very powerful in teaching youngsters positive habits.

Many of our activities are done for a reason; they have a payoff or desirable consequences. We work for money, we dress for approval, we are nice to our bosses so that our bosses will be nice to us. Some psychologists claim that virtually all of our activities are directed by consequences. When we are hungry, the obvious payoff is food, and when we are thirsty, we seek water. We stop eating and drinking after they no longer meet our needs, or no longer provide a payoff.

There are many things that we don't do because doing them can lead to punishment; that is, they produce a negative payoff or consequence. We don't go through red lights, we don't tell our bosses our real opinion of them, we don't steal things we want from stores. We avoid certain unnecessary risks like playing ball on highways for fear of the risk of negative consequences, a punishment: that of being in a serious accident.

Among the first psychologists to study reinforcement was Edward Thorndike. Around 1910, Thorndike studied the problem-solving skills of animals. He placed a hungry cat in a box. The cat had to learn to find and pull a looped string to open the box and get at food. At first the cat wandered aimlessly. Soon, being a cat, it became interested in playing with the string. Lo and behold, when it pulled the loop, the door opened and it got at food. In a short time, the cat learned that pulling the string allowed it to get food. When hungry, it pulled the string increasingly sooner after entering the box. Thorndike resisted the temptation to say that the cat understood what it was doing; he stated only that [solving the problem] several times and getting food stamped in the connection between pulling the string and getting at the food. The cat increased the number of times it pulled the string when it was reinforced by food for doing so.

The psychologist most associated with principles of reinforcement is B.F. Skinner. Skinner studied the behavior of animals under the controlled conditions of a chamber containing a lever. That chamber later became known as the "Skinner Box." Skinner conducted experiments to determine how the principles of reinforcement control behavior. He followed Thorndike and proposed a law of reinforcement: a simple law, it states that reinforced behaviors increase in frequency. That is, if a behavior is reinforced, it occurs more often. If a child is praised for doing homework, it is done more often. The reverse was also true, that if a behavior were not reinforced or was punished, it would occur less often. If a child is criticized for doing homework, it will be done less often. Much of human behavior is determined by consequences. Those activities that have a positive consequence are continued, while those behaviors that have none are eventually discontinued. Few of us will work very long at a job without pay. Few of us will continue to dress in a way that generates criticism. However, generally we will work harder when praised—and thereby given a payoff—than when we are criticized, and thereby punished. Homework, like other human activities, is also influenced by consequences.

Individual Definition of Reinforcement

A further clarification of the concept of reinforcement is necessary. In its definition, we italicized "to the individual" to emphasize that people differ in what they experience as positive or negative. The concept of reinforcement is slightly different from the concept of reward. In many cases this difference is vital. Reinforcement is more individually defined than reward. It is defined simply by those events that have the effect of increasing the frequency of the behavior they follow. It is defined by the individual's behavior. For example, if we see that praising the youngster for effort has the effect of increasing the time spent doing homework, then we obviously conclude that the praise reinforced the homework.

In exactly the same manner, if we see a youngster increasingly resist homework when the resistance leads to parental anger, we would call the parents' anger reinforcement. If having the parents become angry increases resistance to homework, their anger is reinforcing the resistance. In many cases, these youngsters want attention and are reinforced even by negative attention (e.g., criticism). They will, in those cases, do more and more behaviors that generate negative attention. Negative attention is a positive consequence to these youngsters. Therefore, according to the law of reinforcement, when we see parents "punishing" youngsters for not doing homework by yelling, screaming, and pulling their hair out, the punishment as defined by the parents is not punishing to the youngster, but is instead reinforcing. The youngster increasingly resists doing homework when being yelled at. Therefore, being yelled at is reinforcing for that youngster. It has the effect of increasing resistance to doing homework. Parents can determine whether their anger is reinforcing or punishing to their youngster by assessing whether it improves or worsens the youngster's homework performance.

Increasing the Effectiveness of Reinforcement

The consequences should be arranged in certain ways to be most effective. Generally, the payoff is most effective if given immediately after the work. When we are praised for an activity months after we have completed it, it does not motivate us nearly as much as hearing the praise immediately after completing the task. Therefore, to the child, the reinforcement of watching television is immediate, while the reinforcement of performing well in school is delayed. Because of this, it is difficult to have a child give up an immediate reinforcer for a delayed one.

Furthermore, we avoid those activities that cost us; i.e., those activities that are punishing. We may know a person who, although charming and fun, frequently borrows money. After being hit by that person a few times, many of us walk the other way when that person is in sight. We have been punished by that person for being nice and we avoid that person. We have also seen several good causes fail because the payoff was negative: either the people working would not see the results of their labor, or they would be charged for their efforts. For example, one group that tried to support handicapped children faded out after its well-meaning leader kept asking members to contribute money or to sell raffles. The members avoided the group after a while. Although they believed in the cause, they were getting "punished" for helping. The punishment of the costs was immediate, while the benefits of doing good were delayed. This is one reason that maintaining diets is difficult for many people; the pleasure of eating occurs considerably before the reward of losing weight. One problem with homework, too, is that the payoff of doing a good job is often delayed, while the "punishment" of interrupting play or simply doing it is more immediate. Many habits that people wish to break are reinforced immediately and punished later. We must take care that youngsters with poor homework habits are not reinforced for their poor habits immediately and reinforced in a delayed manner for their positive habits.

Dangers of Punishment When Applied to Homework

Obviously, the implications of this simple law for the doing of homework are enormous. If homework were reinforced, it would be done more often. If it were punished, it would be done less often.

Imagine that we want to train a dog to come when it hears the command of a whistle. At first the dog responds slowly and sometimes not at all. If an owner became angry at the dog and hit it for being slow, that dog would be foolish to come to that master. Any self-respecting dog would think, "He's going to hit me for coming when he whistles, and I don't need that!" However, if we petted and praised even when the dog dawdles, the dog would come faster each time. The response of going to the person whistling would be reinforced, by the stroking and praising. In the same way, when parents yell at children that their homework is done sloppily, that they shouldn't dawdle or that they should be happy to have homework, the youngster would be crazy NOT to avoid doing homework. Homework has become associated with yelling and screaming.

Skinner also stated that punishment was a very ineffective way to "stamp out" unwanted behaviors. Indeed, throughout this book we will not advocate the use of any punishment in the teaching of good homework habits. Skinner found that punishment led to unwanted side effects in learning. The animal would become emotional, and this interfered with learning. In the case of children, it is considerably more intense. Children often become emotional, usually angry, when they are punished. Anger not only interferes with learning, it can be an intense incentive for defiance. We therefore present a method of winning the homework war with love, not with weapons. The use of punishment is not advocated. The parent should also be aware of conditions that are punishing to their child so that the punishment can be eliminated.

Shaping

An important principle in the use of reinforcement is that of *shaping*, a useful way to speed the development of homework habits. Shaping is the reinforcing of small steps toward a goal. By using shaping, reinforcement is given as the youngster gets nearer to the desired behavior. It means that reinforcement is given when there is progress toward the goal, and not necessarily when the child has reached the goal.

Going back to the dog-training example, if the dog was reinforced by petting, praise, or food for coming when called, even when it dawdled, the dog would return. Soon, the trainer would give the reinforcers only when the dog came somewhat faster. Each time, the dog would be reinforced for coming faster than the previous time; the dog's behavior would slowly be "shaped" so that the dog came immediately upon being called.

We once gave our classes a devious example to demonstrate the power of shaping. We asked the students to smile and act attentive when their professor was standing on the right-hand half of the classroom and look away when the professor was at the left-hand half. Watching a class smile and be attentive is very reinforcing to most college professors. When the professor began to spend more time at the right side, the class was instructed to then smile when the instructor was in the right-hand quarter and look away when the professor was in the left three-quarters of the classroom. Finally, the class was asked to smile and act attentive only while the professor was in the right-hand corner of the classroom. Students have reported that it works — that professors, without actually being aware of it, have been shaped to teach in the right-hand corner.

This example demonstrates the critical principle of shaping. In order to be effective, shaping must start from where the person "is." Most professors will wander while teaching. If the class began smiling when the professor was in the corner, shaping would take forever because the professor would rarely be in the corner and there would be little opportunity for reinforcement. By beginning at a spot that the professor actually occupies, the procedure is made more efficient. When we discuss the use of shaping your youngster to develop better homework habits, it will be important for you to pinpoint where the youngster is, and not where he or she should be.

Intermittent Reinforcement

So far we have discussed the need for consistency on the part of the parent in order to help the youngster develop better homework habits. We stress consistency to highlight yet another important principle of learning: the law of *Intermittent Reinforcement.* Although this sounds difficult, it is not. The law holds that those behaviors that are irregularly reinforced (reinforced intermittently) are difficult to eliminate compared to those that are *never* reinforced. It is essentially an all-or-nothing law. Therefore, when your child asks to be allowed to watch the end of a television program when it is homework time, your child should be told that he or she can watch only after the homework is finished. If you are inconsistent and allow your child to watch some times and not others, intermittent reinforcement occurs. It will, therefore, be harder for you to have your child do homework during the designated time. Be consistent!

The compulsive gambler is one example of how intense irregularly or intermittently reinforced behaviors can become. Compulsive gamblers are almost always on an intermittent reinforcement pattern:

they win sometimes and lose sometimes. Because of the intermittent reinforcement, gamblers develop a habit of gambling that is very difficult to stop. If gamblers won all the time and then lost *all* the time, they would learn that they were not going to win and it would be easier to quit. However, to gamblers, winning seems to be just around the corner because it has been just around the corner before. They therefore continue to gamble despite knowing that gambling is destructive. Similarly, the youngster who is intermittently reinforced for poor homework habits does not know that he or she is a victim of the history of reinforcement. These behaviors are not purposeful, but are products of reinforcement histories. Our job is to use principles of reinforcement to help the youngster develop better and more productive homework habits.

Review of Principles

Let us review the principles of reinforcement and how they contribute to bad homework habits. The first principle is that reinforcement increases the behavior it follows. Which of your youngster's homework habits do you wish to increase? How can you go about reinforcing those homework habits? Are you reinforcing your youngster with praise for attempting homework? Are you reinforcing your youngster with negative attention for not doing homework? Remember that reinforcement is more effective when delivered immediately after the behaviors we wish to reinforce.

The second principle is that punishment decreases the behaviors it follows. Are you engaging in behaviors that could be punishing your child for doing home-work? Are you punishing your child by criticism for attempting homework? Could you be inadvertently denigrating your youngster's efforts to do homework? Do you hear yourself saying things like, "Is this piece of junk the best you could do?" Could you be punish-ing behaviors that you wish to increase?

The third principle is shaping, or reinforcing gradual approximation to the goal of good homework habits. Do you expect your youngster to develop good homework habits all at once? Remember, it is easy for parents to say that their youngster should be able to do half an hour's homework without getting up. However, for your youngster this goal may be entirely unrealistic. You must reinforce the youngster just for doing better, even if that means sitting down for two minutes in the beginning. Next, the time expected can be three minutes, and so on. The youngster can-not be reinforced for thirty minutes of work, because that is much longer than his or her initial capacities. Desired behavior must be shaped.

The last principle is the law of intermittent rein-forcement. Here, consistency is critical. If a youngster is reinforced haphazardly for poor homework habits, then it will become difficult to rid that youngster of poor habits. For example, if Charlie is occasionally allowed to play with his video games during home-work time, he has been intermittently reinforced for not doing homework. That intermittent reinforce-ment will make it harder for Charlie to develop stable homework patterns.

We have just given you principles and ideas that, we assume, are different from what you have been using. Many parents will resist reinforcing behaviors that are not up to the expected standard. We want parents to shape positive homework skills in steps, not all at once. Parents resist, saying, "Even though homework is better than before, it is still sloppy. How can I praise Jimmy for it? Why shouldn't he just do it right?" We usually ask the parents whether they have tried it their way. Then we ask if punishing a child who has poor homework habits has worked. They admit that they get only heartburn from punishing. We ask them to remember that being right is easy but that the principles we want them to try have proven effective. They will require parents to try a new approach.

In the next chapters we shall give more detail on how to use the principles of reinforcement and the principles of association to develop better homework habits in your child.

4

Pinpointing Your Child's
Specific Homework Problems

In Chapter 1, we presented a variety of homework problems commonly encountered by parents and children. Some youngsters have organization problems, some daydream, while others may simply be negative and resist any attempt to get them to do homework (or chores, or even to play). Obviously, different problems require different solutions.

The Homework Problem Checklist

Shoiock, O'Leary, and Anesko have developed a Homework Problem Checklist that will help you identify the specific type of problem or problems that your youngster is having. The checklist items were selected on the basis of many interviews with parents, teachers, and clinicians who work with children. They were asked to list common homework problems that youngsters have. At this time we would like you to complete the checklist, on pages 47-50. Read each statement and indicate how often your child has that problem by checking off "never," "at times," "often," or "very often." When in doubt, give the answer that first comes to mind and be certain to answer each item.

To determine how much of a problem you and your child are having with homework, score the checklist by counting the checkmarks. Each checkmark in the "never" column is equal to 0 points, each "at times" response equals 1 point, "often" is 2 points, and "very often" is 3 points. After scoring in this manner, add the total for each response category to arrive at an overall score.

Homework Problem Checklist

FOR EACH STATEMENT CHECK ONE:	NEVER (0)	AT TIMES (1)	OFTEN (2)	VERY OFTEN (3)
1 Fails to bring home assignment and necessary materials (textbook, dittos, etc.)				
2 Doesn't know exactly what homework has been assigned				
3 Denies having homework assignment				
4 Refuses to do homework assignment				
5 Whines or complains about homework				
6 Must be reminded to sit down and start homework				
7 Procrastinates, puts off doing homework				

FOR EACH STATEMENT CHECK ONE:	NEVER (0)	AT TIMES (1)	OFTEN (2)	VERY OFTEN (3)
8 Doesn't do homework satisfactorily unless someone is in the room				
9 Doesn't do homework satisfactorily unless someone does it with him/her (like Marcie or Chuck)				
10 Daydreams or plays with objects during homework session				
11 Easily distracted by noises or activities of others				
12 . Easily frustrated by homework assignment				
13 Fails to complete homework				
14 Takes unusually long time to do homework				
15 Responds poorly when told by parent to correct homework				
16 Produces messy or sloppy homework				
17 Hurries through homework and makes careless mistakes				
18 Shows dissatisfaction with work, even when he/she does a good job				
19 Forgets to bring assignment to class				
20 Deliberately fails to bring assignment back to class				
TOTAL SCORE				

Here's an example of how the checklist might be completed for Charlie Brown's friend Peppermint Patti, a cartoon-character famous for her homework-related trials and tribulations.

FOR EACH STATEMENT CHECK ONE:	NEVER (0)	AT TIMES (1)	OFTEN (2)	VERY OFTEN (3)
1 Fails to bring home assignment and necessary materials (textbook, dittos, etc.)				X
2 Doesn't know exactly what homework has been assigned				X
3 Denies having homework assignment	X			
4 Refuses to do homework assignment	X			
5 Whines or complains about homework		X		
6 Must be reminded to sit down and start homework			X	
7 Procrastinates, puts off doing homework			X	
8 Doesn't do homework satisfactorily unless someone is in the room		X		
9 Doesn't do homework satisfactorily unless someone does it with him/her (like Marcie or Chuck)		X		
10 Daydreams or plays with objects during homework session				X
11 Easily distracted by noises or activities of others			X	

FOR EACH STATEMENT CHECK ONE:	NEVER (0)	AT TIMES (1)	OFTEN (2)	VERY OFTEN (3)
12 Easily frustrated by homework assignment		X		
13 Fails to complete homework			X	
14 Takes unusually long time to do homework			X	
15 Responds poorly when told by parent to correct homework		X		
16 Produces messy or sloppy homework				X
17 Hurries through homework and makes careless mistakes		X		
18 Shows dissatisfaction with work, even when he/she does a good job		X		
19 Forgets to bring assignment to class				X
20 Deliberately fails to bring assignment back to class		X		
TOTAL SCORE	0+	8+	10+	15=33

The overall checklist score can be used to learn the degree of difficulty that your child is having with homework in comparison with other youngsters. Actual norms, included below, have been developed for children in second, third, and fourth grades based on checklists completed by over 300 parents.

		GRADE	
	2	3	4
BOYS' SCORES			
Average	12	13	12
Some Problems	20	22	21
Many Problems	28	32	30
GIRLS' SCORES			
Average	8	9	10
Some Problems	14	16	18
Many Problems	20	23	26

Although these comparisons will be less direct for older children, they will be helpful for a rough comparison of your child with others. If your child earns a score at or lower than the average score for homework problems, that means your child is having fewer problems with homework than most youngsters. It does not mean that there is no room for improvement. For example, if your child "fails to complete homework", (item 13) and does not score highly on other items, he or she still has a significant homework problem. Not all the questions are of equal importance. Even a low score can indicate the need for development of better homework habits. On the other hand, if your child obtains a high score on the homework checklist, scores at or above those labeled "Many Problems," you require a plan of attack. However, the plan cannot involve telling the youngster what a rotten kid he or she is because of the high score. As we shall discuss later, criticism tends to do more harm than good.

The Most Common Homework Problems

In either case, the checklist can help you to identify categories of homework problems—clusters of homework behaviors that often occur together and respond to the same types of intervention. We have divided the problems into the following categories: *What Homework to do, When to do Homework, Where to do Homework, How to do Homework,* and *Why do Homework.*

What Homework to do

The problems under this category concern the youngster who does not have the correct assignment when it is time to do homework. Items 1, 2, and 19 on the checklist tap these problems. It can, and often does, drive her parents insane when Jennifer gets ready to do homework and says that she can't find her homework assignment. Her parents have been known to grind their teeth to powder as Jennifer rummages through different pockets and different books in search of her work. Sometimes Jennifer finds the assignment, but more often than not she doesn't. This is extremely trying for her parents and for Jennifer, as well as being a waste of time. It also brings a steely glint to her parents' eyes when they are told by Jennifer that she did the homework but forgot to turn it in.

Jennifer is disorganized, and she, as well as her parents, is paying a high price for this disorganization. In addition to the lowering of her school performance, Jennifer's parents are going crazy. They are often angry at her and show their anger. Jennifer is feeling put down and gets down on herself. Chapter 5 will provide guidelines that Jennifer and her parents can follow to increase the girl's organizational skills.

When to do Homework

Peter sometimes completes his homework. He says that he should do it when he comes home from school, but often the kids in the neighborhood ask him to play street hockey. Of course he would rather play street hockey. Sometimes he even starts the work after he comes home but then hears the sounds of a touch football game. Touch football is more fun than homework, too. Peter then eats dinner after he plays and fully intends to do his homework after dinner. However, he realizes that his favorite television program is on and that he can always do his homework after the program is over. After all, the program is only an hour long.

At this point, Peter's parents get into the act. They first gently remind him that he should do his homework first. Peter thinks that they don't understand that his favorite program will be over by the time he does his homework. Why couldn't he just do it as soon as the program is over? Peter's parents begin to get mad. They have heard this "solution" again and again and have learned that after the favorite program comes the next favorite. The fight begins.

The *When to do Homework* questions, checklist items 6, 7, 8, and 9, underscore the absence of a routine that would signal the time to begin homework. These items also refer to homework practices in which the parents must constantly prod the youngster to keep at the work. Some students who resist beginning homework will also not keep at it unless they are under strict surveillance by their parents. For example, Eric will stop homework within a fraction of a second after his parents leave the room. Although Eric appears to be working, his parents are always amazed that not one bit of work is completed when they are not in the room.

Where to do Homework

Michelle is full of surprises. Sometimes she does homework in the kitchen and sometimes at her desk. Then, when certain television programs are on, she is able to do the work while watching television. There are even times when she does her homework on the floor with her feet leaning on the couch. The *Where to do Homework* checklist questions overlap somewhat with the "when to do. . ." items and include entries 8, 9, 10, 11, and 14.

Michelle's parents have tried to encourage her to do homework in a single spot, but she resists. Doing homework in one place doesn't make sense to her. She prefers doing several things at once, like watching T.V. and chatting with her family, while doing her homework. If the homework were finished, Michelle's parents wouldn't care where she did it. The problem is that she becomes distracted and the homework does not get done. Chapter 6 will focus on methods to assist parents and children in developing an effective homework routine that includes setting a time and a place for homework completion, and will also provide tips on how to organize the work area to make studying easier.

How to do Homework

Karen is an eight-year-old who finishes most assignments and often gets easy questions correct. However, her work is done only under the close supervision of her parents, older brother, or babysitter. It's not that she has to be prodded to start the work, it's just that as soon as her parents or brother leave the room, Karen calls for more help or will carry her assignment out to her folks, saying, "I don't know how to do this" or "What do I do next?" Her teacher reports that Karen works best in one-to-one activities where she has the undivided attention of the teacher or teacher's aide to help her set up the problems. Despite Karen's reliance on others for help with her work, her test results indicate that she's a child of at least average intelligence who displays no known learning disabilities.

If your child earns scores of 2 or more on checklist items 2, 5, 6, 7, 8, 9, 12, and 18, he or she may have problems that fall into the category of *How to do Homework*. Chapter 7 focuses on developing in such children skills in reading and following instructions, breaking problems into smaller steps to arrive at final solutions, setting homework goals with parents, and rewarding themselves for trying hard. Parents will find out how they can use their attention and praise to teach their children how to work more independently and develop greater self-confidence in their academic abilities.

Why do Homework

This category of behaviors applies to children with motivational problems. These youngsters often fall into two groups: those who actively resist doing homework and are defiant, and those who could care less about school. The defiant youngsters are usually angry with their parents or with the school and generally will earn high scores on checklist items 3, 4, 12, 15, and 20. However, angry students can express their feelings in a remarkable variety of ways so that all items can reflect the behavior of a defiant youngster.

Richard was one rebellious fourteen-year-old who developed wonderful revenge tactics to use with his parents. They wanted him to do well in school and insisted that he do homework every day after supper. Richard told them that he thought this was a good idea and that he would follow their suggestions. However, after the second day, Richard said that he would start his work later in the evening. His parents reminded him of the agreement and then tried to explain that it was for his own good. After discussion proved fruitless, they embarked on their own strategy of revenge. "You can't watch T.V. until you do your homework!" When that failed, they escalated their threats: "You're grounded for the weekend because you didn't do homework!" Richard, in turn, just stopped telling his parents that he had homework and instead said that he had finished the work at school. Later, notes from his teachers informed the parents that the homework was not being done. Richard's parents thought about the possibility of applying for a child-abuse permit.

Donna, on the other hand, just doesn't seem to care that she does poorly in school. She and other youngsters like her will probably score high on items 1, 5, 7, 16, 17, and 19. She does her homework in the fastest possible time even though it is sloppy and incorrect. She will redo it when her parents indicate that it needs to be redone, but is annoyed at the inconvenience. Her parents have explained that it is important to do homework, and she listens, but is just not interested in the work.

In most cases, youngsters with homework problems evidence behaviors from each of the categories we have described. The student who is indifferent to homework often is also angry because he or she doesn't understand why so much pressure is being exerted to complete something—he or she believes—as unimportant as homework. The youngster who is disorganized may also have motivational problems because of a long record of poor school performance. Often these children have been so severely criticized for so long that they believe themselves to be as "bad" or "dull" as they have been told they are, and are therefore less inclined to put forth much effort when it comes to doing homework.

Talking to the Teacher

Once you've completed the Homework Problem Checklist and identified particular aspects of the homework process that are troublesome to you and your child, it's probably time to consult with your child's teacher. Are there patterns of poor work habits that also show up at school? Information about your child's classroom performance can be essential to a complete assessment of his or her homework problems. Is your son or daughter defiant? A child who argues with the teacher? Or might he or she be viewed as passive or indifferent? Does the youngster seem to care about school work? Is he or she disorganized? How well does your child get along with classmates? In several instances we discovered boys and girls who were being teased by other children and who thus found school punishing. We have also seen cases in which a youngster tried to impress peers with a show of toughness by doing poorly in school. Unless you speak to the teacher, you may not be aware of these pressures your child faces.

Analyzing the Home Situation

An assessment of your youngster's homework problems is not complete until you have taken a close look at your own behavior. Believe it or not, parents' attitudes and actions often contribute to making homework more of a hardship for all involved. For example, some mothers and fathers whose children's homework checklist scores fall within the combined categories of "what homework and when and where to do it" are often disorganized and overloaded with daily responsibilities, thus setting ineffective examples for their children. Such parents might ask themselves: "Have I been successful in establishing routines in my family's life [e.g., set meal times, chores, scheduled activities, etc.]?" "Do the time demands and responsibilities I'm faced with disrupt my child's homework schedule [e.g., do you interrupt study time to have the child run errands, babysit, take phone calls, sit near you so that you can supervise even though you're cooking or cleaning, etc.]?" "Is our home set up so that a study area is available that is quiet, well lit, and comfortably furnished?"

Youngsters with *Why do Homework* problems often have parents whose anger and impatience set the stage for what we call "warfare in the family." In cases like these, the parents get involved in a struggle in which their goal is to control their son or daughter, and they often resort to coercion to achieve this goal. The child in turn feels, justifiably, that "my parents are always on my back" and may retaliate by doing poorly as a way to assert his or her "freedom" from parental direction. Mom and Dad continue to stay angry, often feeling that they must remain so in order not to condone irresponsible behavior, and often increase threats and punishment. This vicious cycle results not only in the buildup of resentment between parent and child but also in an increased investment, by both sides, in not losing this "homework war." But, as in all wars, there are no winners, only losers. Nevertheless, parents can take steps to "negotiate a truce" if they're first willing to acknowledge their role in maintaining the conflict surrounding homework.

Parents, knowingly and unknowingly, can also convey attitudes and expectations about homework or their child's ability to handle it that serve to undermine his or her motivation to complete assignments. Sometimes statements are made that imply that the homework or the teacher is not to be taken seriously. For example, how might you feel if you, as a child, heard your parents say any of the following:

"Let me show you a better way to do this multiplication problem than the one Mrs. Smith showed you."

"No, we can't go to the library tonight for those books. Your report will have to wait until the weekend."

"Sorry for interrupting you when you're doing your

homework, but I've got a lot of errands to run. Watch your sister for me while I'm gone."

"This is nothing but busy work—doesn't Mr. Jones know that you already know how to do fractions?"

"You're reading that book for your book report? It's pretty boring, if you ask me."

It may be true that you sometimes question the value of the work that has been assigned, or disagree with the method of approaching the work taught by the teacher, or perhaps you and your child's teacher just aren't fond of one another. For the most part, however, you'll need to keep these opinions to yourself to avoid teaching your child that homework and/or the teacher are to be disregarded. Or you might wish to find a more appropriate person to listen to your concerns—namely, your child's teacher. Improving communication between home and school is emphasized throughout this book as one effective means of reducing homework-related problems. Chapters 5, 7, 8, and 10 provide specific suggestions you can follow to pinpoint your child's homework strengths and weaknesses from the teacher's perspective, identify the teacher's goals for homework, and clarify your role in the homework process.

Attacking the Problem

Now, given the information you've collected from the Homework Problem Checklist, your child's teacher, and your assessment of the expectations and attitudes you hold about homework, you're ready to choose a homework problem to tackle first. Rather than be haphazard and attack all problems at once, the simplest approach involves reviewing the checklist items on pages 47-48 to select one or two problems for change. The problems chosen should be the ones that are causing the greatest difficulty for your child and are occurring most of the time when homework is assigned. You'll want to start with a good description of the homework problem, one that clearly spells out what difficulties your child is having and under what circumstances they occur. So, for example, rather than just get frustrated and say that "Toni is a lazy oaf," the parent must be a careful observer of the child's behavior. When we talk about how homework is usually done, we frequently get answers like, "George makes careless mistakes when doing homework." A far more useful definition of the homework problem is one that is nonevaluative and unemotional, an objective description such as this: "George gets less than 50 percent of his math problems correct even after I ask him to check over his work."

In another case, the parent reported that Maggie "just couldn't sit still." When asked to describe what she meant by this, the mother replied, "Maggie went to her room to do homework and got up and went to the refrigerator twelve minutes later. She sat for five minutes and then wanted water. After returning for four minutes, she went to the bathroom. She got up seventy-two times in ninety-eight minutes." Why is this detail important? Without details like how long something lasts or how often something occurs, you may make two mistakes that can interfere with your successful use of the programs described in this book. First of all, you may incorrectly decide that something your child is doing (or not doing, as the case may be) is a problem and should be changed.

For example, Mrs. Santelli believed that her son, Enrico, took an unusually long time to do his homework. She guessed that he spent well over the hour that his teacher felt was reasonable for the amount of work assigned. So, she would scold him for being so slow and pop into his room every five minutes to be sure that he continued working. But no matter what she did, Enrico continued to work at about the same rate, saying he was working as fast as he could. Mrs. Santelli finally decided that, rather than stay constantly frustrated with her son, she'd time him to see how long it actually took Enrico to finish his assignments each night. She was surprised (and embarrassed) to discover that her son spent about forty to fifty minutes studying. She had, in fact, not seen the homework situation accurately. What she thought was a homework problem really wasn't one.

Other parents make the mistake of assuming that their child's homework program isn't working, without keeping records of how often the troublesome behavior(s) occurred *before* and *after* they intervened. Let's refer back to Maggie, the girl who "couldn't sit still." If Maggie's mother hadn't counted the number of times her daughter was out of her seat during homework sessions before starting one of the programs in this book, she might suppose that no improvement had occurred when, after a week of programming, she counted twenty-four times that Maggie left her seat. In comparison with her first count of seventy-two instances of leaving the desk before she and her mother started their homework program, Maggie was now out of her seat only one-third the times. That was a positive change that Maggie's mother was able to recognize.

So, before you try to change a homework problem you must:

(1) Define or describe the problem behavior so that you can
    a) Observe it—that is, see it or hear it.
    b) Measure it—count how often it happens or how long it lasts.

Your definition should be clear and specific so that another person (husband, wife, teacher, tutor, etc.) would know exactly what behavior you were referring to if he or she were to observe your child's homework session.

The following are some examples of behavior descriptions; you decide whether or not they meet the requirements of a good behavior definition. If not, try to write out a definition that does satisfy the guidelines listed above.

a) being lazy _____

_____

b) reading a book _____

_____

c) getting angry _____

_____

d) daydreaming _____

_____

e) doing math
   problems

_____

_____

If you thought that a, c, and d were behaviors that would be hard to observe and measure, you're right! While it's true that each of us has a picture in mind of someone "being lazy," "getting angry," or "daydreaming," if we compared pictures we'd find that these behaviors mean different things to different people. By comparison, b and e describe behaviors that can be easily seen, agreed upon, and measured by two or more people. You can see someone's eyes moving along as they read the words printed in a book or watch the pages being turned. You can count the number of math problems that are solved and watch the pencil write the calculations.

"But my child *does* get angry when he's doing his homework!" "My child daydreams constantly," you might protest. "These are problems we want to work on." Fine—all we ask is that you describe what your child says or does when you refer to him or her as "angry." For example, does your child shout, cry, curse, slam books to the floor, say, "I'm not doing this anymore," pound his/her fist on the desk, frown, or stamp his/her feet? Describing "angry" in clear, specific, observable terms will enable you to measure how often it happens. Likewise, when your child "daydreams," does he or she stare out the window, doodle on paper, watch his/her pet hamster move in its cage, shoot paper airplanes across the room, gaze at the picture of the current boyfriend or girlfriend, and so on? These are behaviors that we can see, hear, and count.

Describing and Observing the Problem

Now it's your turn. Describe each problem behavior you and your child have decided to change so that you can observe whether it occurs daily. Write your specific, concrete problem-behavior descriptions below:

PROBLEM BEHAVIOR #1: _____

_____

PROBLEM BEHAVIOR #2: _____

_____

(2) Observe for at least one week how often each behavior happens on the days your child has homework.

Now that you've described the behaviors you'd like to change, the next step is to determine how often they're occurring now. This information is needed so that you can be sure that you've correctly identified homework problems. This record of observations will also represent what is known as a **baseline**, the rate at which a behavior occurs naturally, before you and your child introduce a program to handle homework differently. While making these observations, try hard not to change just yet the ways in which you deal with your child over homework. This baseline record of observations provides you and your child with a starting point for setting realistic homework goals because it represents your child's current level of functioning or performance. This notion of setting goals will be discussed in more detail in Chapter 7. Once you and your child begin a program to strengthen good homework habits, we'll again ask you to keep records of how often each problem homework behavior occurs to see if the program is working.

Now you're ready to watch and record how often your child's problem homework behaviors arise. After reviewing the following sample charts, fill in the chart that follows them. After you define the problem behavior so that you can observe it, place a check in the appropriate box; "occurred" or "didn't occur." Also indicate, if possible, how many times it happened during each homework session or, when appropriate, how long the behavior lasted (e.g., "stared out the window for five minutes," "waited fifteen minutes before starting homework after being reminded to begin"). You might also indicate whether or not homework was assigned.

EXAMPLES

PROBLEM BEHAVIOR: Denise must be reminded several times before she will start her homework.

	MONDAY	TUESDAY	WEDNESDAY	THURSDAY	FRIDAY
Occurred	√		√	√	
Didn't occur		√			√
How often? How long?	5 reminders		2 reminders	4 reminders	no homework

PROBLEM BEHAVIOR: Andrew spends less than the 20 minutes required by his teacher on his reading each night.

	MONDAY	TUESDAY	WEDNESDAY	THURSDAY	FRIDAY
Occurred	√	√			
Didn't occur			√	√	√
How long? How often?	Read for 10 min.	Didn't read	Read for 30 min.	Read for 20 min.	Read for 30 min.

Now you try it. Please make your observations daily for the next week.

PROBLEM BEHAVIOR: _____

	MONDAY	TUESDAY	WEDNESDAY	THURSDAY	FRIDAY
Occurred					
Didn't occur					
How often? How long?					

5

Getting Homework Home

It comes as a surprise to some parents to learn that their son or daughter's poor report card marks can be attributed to the youngster's failure to complete all assigned homework and/or to turn in the right assignments. They recall either seeing their child hard at work or being told that no work was assigned that day. They may also remember the last-minute phone calls to classmates spent trying to figure out what problems would be due in math class the next day, and the anguished pleas to "drive me back to school" when the child discovered he or she had left the social studies books or spelling list in his or her locker. If these situations sound familiar, your child probably earned scores of 2 or more on items 1, 2, and 3 of the Homework Problem Checklist. He or she will benefit from help designed to increase the rate at which all necessary homework materials, including written assignments, actually get home on time, and not one or two days later.

It is extremely frustrating when parents who are in a good mood and eager to help say to their youngsters "Let's do homework together now" and the children reply sheepishly that they forgot to bring home their assignments. The parent often will say, "But we talked about assignments this morning and you said that you would remember to bring them home!" The youngster usually agrees but maintains that he or she forgot. At this point most parents lose their sense of humor. It is not unknown for them to grit their teeth, to mutter under their breath or out loud how they have been cursed with an incurable problem and how they wish children just like theirs on their own children. Instead, let's analyze the problem and look for ways to help.

First, it is important that you and the teacher remain in close contact about what type and amount of homework is usual for your child. You might wish to schedule such a meeting several weeks after school starts. By that time the teacher will have introduced regular homework assignments (e.g., spelling test on Friday, vocabulary words on Monday, math problems every night, etc.). Approach this meeting with the teacher with an attitude that both of you are partners in an alliance to help your child. You should say something like, "Johnny has a problem remembering to bring his homework home and we want to help him remember. What can I do to help?" Avoid criticizing Johnny (e.g., "What am I going to do about that rotten kid? He drives me crazy!") and avoid criticizing the teacher (e.g., "Why haven't you told me that Johnny isn't handing in his homework?"). Remember, your goal is to help Johnny bring home his assignments, not to prove that he's a terrible child or that the teacher is at fault. You must think in terms of dealing with the problem: *"How can we help Johnny bring his assignments home?"*

After talking to the teacher, you should have a pretty good idea of the amount and type of homework your child gets and how often such work is assigned. At this point, it is important that you communicate this information to Johnny. Reducing the payoffs for not completing work should not involve punishment, because it produces the opposite effect of what we want. When Johnny is punished for not doing homework, Johnny will find ways of avoiding punishment. Not telling the truth is a common way of avoiding punishment (or at least delaying it). Thus, you might hear Johnny say that the teacher doesn't give homework on Tuesdays or that today was declared a "non-homework day" to celebrate the middle of the basketball season, or some other imaginative story. If Johnny knows that you know *what* homework to expect when, he will realize that you are that much harder to fool and will be less likely to try such tactics.

Determining the specific resistance to homework your child is displaying is the next step in increasing the chances that homework will get home. We've encountered several reasons for youngsters having trouble. Among the most common is that the student does not write down the assignment when it is given by the teacher. Claudia is like that; she doesn't write down the assignment and yet honestly expects to remember it when the time for homework arrives each evening. Unfortunately, by that time Claudia is often embarrassed after realizing that she has forgotten what she's supposed to do. Although there are times when she does recall all assignments, most of the time she forgets some of the work. Then Claudia runs frantically to the phone, hoping her friends will be able to give her the correct assignments. When they do, she is relieved and goes about doing her homework. When she can't reach a classmate, she may tell her parents that she did not have much homework. She may even think she had little to do until the next day, when she is in the classroom and the teacher tells the class to pass in the work for grading.

Claudia has developed a poor work habit—she thinks that she can remember the homework without writing it down. The homework assignments are so clear to her the moment after they are given that Claudia cannot imagine not remembering them later. Very often this habit develops because homework assignments were usually very simple in the early grades and Claudia could then get by by relying on just her memory. However, as the work gets more complicated as the child gets older, so, too, do the homework requirements. A good memory is often not sufficient for recalling all assignments. The bad habits have already been developed and are contributing to Claudia's problem.

Tracy, on the other hand, will jot down assignments occasionally. However, there are times when she has better things to do than writing down her assignments—for example, when her girlfriend whispers to her about the new stickers she's bought, or when the cute new boy looks her way and smiles. These activities make it hard for her to concentrate on what the teacher is saying. It's not surprising, then, that Tracy doesn't always know what she's to do for homework when her parents ask.

In contrast, Kenny faithfully writes down each assignment. He writes some on the back of ditto sheets, some on his assignment pad, and some on scraps of paper. With all these papers to keep in order, Kenny often finds that he's lost one or more of the assignments. He spends a great deal of valuable time trying to retrieve the misplaced work, crying to his parents "I know I wrote it down!" when they ask "Where are your assignments, Kenny?" When he doesn't find his notes, he too, like Claudia, must call friends for guidance or opt not to do the work.

Like Claudia and Kenny, many youngsters have developed study habits that become ineffective and detrimental as homework becomes more complicated. Kenny was able to write assignments on bits of paper and still do adequately in the early grades. Homework was simple, and a more systematic approach to tackling it was not needed then. Now, however, these habits, which did no harm then, are not useful and in fact create problems. In the cases of Claudia and Kenny, the job of their parents will be to help them develop better skills in recording assignments and then making sure the assignments reach home at the end of each day.

Ronald is another youth who fails to bring assignments home, but for reasons other than those that apply to Kenny, Claudia, and Tracy. When Ronald's parents finally get him to "find" his assignments, he still resists doing homework. Misplacing his homework is just one of several methods the boy has developed to avoid doing the assignments. Ronald will score high on other items from the Homework Problem Checklist, including "must be reminded to start the work," "procrastinates," "produces messy work," and "forgets to bring assignments back to school." Despite these other problem areas, getting Ronald's homework home is the starting point for mastering (or at least improving) his study skills.

Finally, some children, like Frank, will either forget the assignment or forget to bring home the books and papers needed to complete it. Frank will sit down at his desk, carefully read his assignment, and then call out, "Mom, have you seen my English book?" With a sigh, his mother starts the search for the book. Sometimes she's successful and the book is found. More often than not, Frank eventually recalls that he left it in his locker at school. Now he must track down a classmate nearby who'll lend him the textbook. Sometimes he's successful but other times he's not, and as a result the work is not completed. Not remembering to bring home all necessary homework materials becomes a more common problem the older the child gets and the more classes he or she takes. Some of the typical excuses a parent might hear include: "I didn't have time to go to my locker before I got on the bus," "I can't carry all those books—they're too heavy," or "I left my Spanish book at the assembly last period."

All of these youngsters present frustrating problems for themselves, their parents, and their teachers. Parents must first ask themselves what approaches have already been tried to remedy the homework problems and then determine how effective (or ineffective) they have been. Parents usually dislike feeling helpless, as when Frank, for example, says, "I really want to do my homework. I can't help it if I forgot my assignment." The parents' frustration can be compounded by their being unable to retrieve the homework materials needed for Frank and having to sit and watch while Frank doesn't get his homework done. So they find themselves falling back on punishment-oriented approaches like yelling, threatening, withholding privileges, and cursing at Frank. If these approaches worked, we would recommend them to our readers. In Frank's case they haven't worked, and his parents need to try a new approach. They can tell themselves that they have a right to be angry. Perhaps they do. However, the goal of this book is not to be right but to be effective. If yelling, threatening, and grounding the boy have not worked, it's time to try something new, like the approaches based on the psychological principles we described in Chapter 3.

Solutions to Getting Homework Home

Let's break down the homework process into smaller steps to see where we can offer useful suggestions to the parents of children described above. The most important step in getting homework home is writing down the assignments as the teacher gives them. This may sound simpler than it is. Teachers vary in the ways that they announce homework. Some write the assignments on the blackboard throughout the day, so that by the end of the day one section of the blackboard has a record of all work due. A child who has trouble seeing the board, who takes a long time to copy written instructions, or who was daydreaming when the assignment was first made is not penalized in such a classroom. As long as he or she remembers to look at the homework board before the day's end, the student can find out what assignments have been given. Most teachers who write assignments on the board, however, erase them shortly afterward. Unless the youngster is paying attention at the time and copies what the teacher has written, some assignments will escape him or her. Parents will need to stress the importance of recording assignments *as* they are given, and should begin to encourage their children to write down assignments as soon as homework becomes part of the child's school experience. This applies also to times when teachers tell the class what work should be done but do not write this information on the board. If your child has trouble writing down what the teacher wants for homework, suggest that he or she ask the teacher to repeat the assignment. While it may feel somewhat embarrassing to ask a teacher to go over an assignment a second time, reassure your youngster that it's better than not understanding what work is expected, and possibly getting what *is* done marked wrong. Assure the youngster that there are other students in the class who didn't get all the information down the first time but who now can do so, thanks to your youngster's request. If your child has particular difficulty writing from dictation (verbal directions), you should make the teacher aware of this, since this problem will affect more than just the student's ability to record homework assignments accurately. In these instances, teachers are often willing to provide children with homework dittos or calendars—sometimes outlining all homework to be completed on a week-by-week basis.

Recording homework assignments is best done by writing down *every* assignment in the *same* book. It is important from the beginning to work this out with your boy or girl. There is no right or wrong place in which to write down assignments so long as they are consistently written down. The usual place for this recording would be either an assignment pad or a notebook. This tablet or notebook will have to travel to and from school every day with your child.

Sit down with Kenny and tell him that you would like to see what can be done to help him avoid some of the problems he is having with bringing assignments home. You know how difficult that makes school for him, and you want to help him avoid getting into additional trouble. You could tell him also that you have been annoyed over the problems he is giving himself and you, and that you want to avoid these fights. You don't need them, and neither does he. It is important that this message be communicated in a spirit of forging an alliance between parent and child. Parents must be very careful not to say, hint, or imply that they are imposing their plan on Claudia. Rather, the plan is worked out through cooperation. This will give Claudia a stake in the changes. The plan will feel much better to all involved when it is worked out *with* rather than *upon* her.

In this same spirit, it is often helpful for Kenny to personalize his notebook or assignment book with decorations. The prouder he is of it and the more he enjoys his notebook, the less likely he is to lose or forget it. If he draws monsters or airplanes, rock stars, or has friends autograph it, it is his and you want him to be proud of it. (We knew one youngster who covered his homework notebook with pictures of Einstein!) This is a point at which you can begin to encourage your boy or girl's involvement with schoolwork. You want to reinforce his or her attention to school, so don't make critical remarks such as "Must you have a Motley Crue insignia on your looseleaf?"; instead, tell Kenny that it looks good (if you can do so with integrity). Avoid developing a critical attitude. Laugh at the latest notebook fashions rather than tell your child how stupid kids are nowadays.

Next, encourage Claudia, Kenny, Tracy, Ronald, and Frank to write down every assignment in their homework book *and in no other place*. We suggest that your child get into the habit of writing down the date the assignment was given, what has to be done, and where the assignment can be found. An example of one child's entry in his "homework log" follows:

DATE	SUBJECT	PAGE	ASSIGNMENT
Tuesday, 3/21	Math	217	Problems 1 to 25
Tuesday, 3/21	Spelling		Learn words for test
Tuesday, 3/21	Reading	30–42	Read story and do questions

Most students seem to prefer to keep homework assignments in small, three-by-five-inch spiral notebooks that fit easily in the pockets of pants, coats, and book bags and thus are convenient to carry. Note pads of this type also provide just enough room to get one day's assignments on a page, thus diminishing the possibility of confusing assignments that are given over two or more days.

Older students will be given weekly (or longer-term) as well as daily assignments. It is critical that they write down when such work is due for at least three reasons: (1) to serve as a reminder that the project has been assigned; (2) to set a deadline for completing the assignment; and (3) to provide a framework for pacing the amount of study time to be devoted to each project. Some students find it helpful to post a list of long-term assignments or to write due dates in large print with brightly colored markers on a calendar hung on the wall above their study area.

When your children do jot down assignments, give them praise and encouragement. By doing so you are using two principles of psychology to develop the habit of bringing assignments home: repetition, or practice, and reinforcement. It is important to direct your attention toward your child's strengths rather than his or her deficiencies. To most youngsters, praise from parents is a very powerful reinforcer. Phrases like "I'm glad that you wrote your assignment down" or "It really saves work when you bring your assignment home" can help to reinforce the development of desirable homework habits. If Johnny brings home most of his assignments but forgets some, reinforce or praise the part that is positive. Remember the principle of *shaping*. We cannot expect Johnny to be a caterpillar one day and a butterfly the next. Changes take time. Be prepared to compliment him for *improvement*. Do not be critical if he is not perfect immediately. Tell Claudia that you are glad she is bringing more homework home and that you hope the improvement continues. Reinforcement (in this case, praise) increases the frequency of the behavior it follows. If you reinforce improvement, you'll see more and more assignments coming home.

As in the case of Ronald's folks, often parents will inadvertently find themselves in a trap where they are reinforcing negative behaviors. This happens in many cases where the youngster is getting more attention for not bringing assignments home than for bringing them home. It is vitally important that your attention be directed at the positive—at those assignments that your youngster *does* bring home. At the same time, it is crucial that less attention be directed at the negative—at those assignments that the youngster fails to bring home. Just say, calmly, that you and your child need to work longer on getting assignments home.

In addition, you may want to provide a little extra help for your son or daughter. Talk to the teacher and ask whether he or she would cooperate and check that Johnny has written down all of his assignments. Ask the teacher to initial the assignment notebook or homework pad at the end of the day to verify that all required work has been written down correctly. The teacher can provide your child with feedback on how well he or she has recorded assignments, saying, for example: "Claudia, I'm glad you wrote down your math assignment, but we still need to work on writing down social studies." This is obviously more encouraging than hearing, "You didn't write down your social studies assignment and you must remember to do so."

Children in elementary school can usually have their assignment books checked by one teacher. When more than one teacher assigns homework, it is important that each teacher initials the assignments he or she has given as well as notes when there are no assignments. Initialing in these cases cuts down on the chances of Frank's parents being suspicious when he says the math teacher didn't give homework. We've included one example of a homework assignment checklist that can be copied onto three-by-five-inch index cards. Each day the student should fill in on one card the work to be done and have the teacher(s) check that the correct assignments have been recorded. Afterward, the card should come home with the youngster as a guide for the completion of that night's schoolwork.

DAILY HOMEWORK RECORD

NAME: _____   DATE: _____

SUBJECT	HOMEWORK ASSIGNED	TEACHER'S SIGNATURE
1. _____	_____	_____
2. _____	_____	_____
3. _____	_____	_____
4. _____	_____	_____
5. _____	_____	_____

You and your child can actually use these cards to measure improvement in the rate at which assignments are written down accurately. Count the number of correct assignments and divide by the total number of assignments given that day. If you then multiply by 100, you'll have the daily percentage of assignments that were correctly recorded. If your child is paying attention when assignments are given, has a homework log to write down what work is due, remembers to take this assignment book home, and is praised by you for these efforts, this daily percentage should increase within the first two to four weeks.

This system could be extended to include notations for how often the child brings home, and/or returns to school, *all* the materials needed to complete assigned work. In the following chart you'll see how Frank's mother worked out a record sheet with the boy to monitor his notes as to one, what to do for each class, and two, what to have with him in order to do it. She also spoke to Frank's teacher, who agreed to inform her of Frank's success (or lack thereof) in both these areas (recording, remembering materials).

DATE: _____

SUBJECT	WHAT TO DO	WHAT I NEED	TEACHER'S COMMENTS
Math	Fractions 1–20	Math ditto	Left ditto in desk
Social Studies	Questions 1-5 on page 50	Social studies book	Took book home
Health	Cut out pictures of 4 food groups	Scissors, magazines	Left on bus

In this example, Frank earned a score of 100 percent for correctly recording all assignments. He had much more trouble when it came to taking necessary homework materials to or from school, as shown by his score of 33 percent. If this pattern of scores continues,

Frank and his mom will need to consider some of the ideas discussed later in this chapter on how to get homework home.

Some students, especially those of junior-and senior-high-school age, are embarrassed by having to get their assignments checked. If your youngster strongly resists this form of monitoring and maintains that he or she can do it without help, you can agree that it's worth giving the suggestion a try. Tell the youngster that if it turns out more help is required to get the work home, you will ask for this assistance from the teacher. If your child succeeds, however, then praise him or her for doing it unassisted.

The parents of children described here can further reduce feelings of frustration by helping their boys and girls to draw up a list of classmates' telephone numbers. No matter how much a youngster paid attention or tried to get back to his or her locker before the bus pulled out, assignments will sometimes be missed or forgotten. Classmates' phone numbers then represent a homework helpline, a means of finding out what work has been assigned and, sometimes, who would be willing to loan your child the book needed to complete the science or history assignment. It's recommended that you have more than one classmate's name and number available so that your child doesn't continually inconvenience the same person. This means that your boy or girl should be willing to return the favor; that is, to provide occasional homework assistance to his or her classmates.

Computer-age approaches to handling lost or forgotten assignments are now being used by a number of school districts throughout the country and will become more and more popular in years to come.

These districts are having teachers enter their homework assignments into the school computers. Youngsters who have computers and modems at home can then call up, access the school computer, and have the assignments appear on their home monitors. You may want to suggest that your school district invest in such a system. It may become standard in the future as more families are able to afford the purchase of personal computers.

Other children, like Frank, may need more assistance because their disorganization spills into many areas of their lives (e.g., the types who forget to tie their shoes). If disorganization is widespread, the child will need extra help in order to get his or her "homework act" together. Signs of the absent-minded child (as opposed to the resistant one) include forgetting to do the things that he or she enjoys, like meeting friends or attending ball games.

The student who tends to forget or misplace materials needed for homework often has no easy way of transporting these papers and/or books. Children in the primary grades can be encouraged to keep homework papers in a special folder—the type that has inside pockets where papers can be inserted and protected. As with the assignment notebooks, the homework folder can be decorated in ways that please the youngster. For example, many folders are available with pictures of popular television, cartoon, and rock music stars. The folder conveniently contains assignments in one central location for travel to and from school. Another device that serves this purpose is a book bag or backpack. Most are waterproof and wear-and-tear resistant. They'll keep papers and books from flying in all directions, and prevent assignments from getting torn or wet. Some boys and girls who are generally forgetful carry the book bag or backpack with them throughout the school day so that they can immediately put aside books and papers needed for homework and not risk mixing them up with those that don't have to come home. The student who has the homework with him or her at all times also cuts down on the chances of accidentally leaving a completed assignment in a locker and having to face the teacher empty-handed.

You can also help an absent-minded Frank by talking to the school and seeing whether Frank can keep an extra set of books at home. Explain that Frank has problems in the area of organization and, despite attempts by both you and Frank, he still forgets his books. Some school districts will be pleased to help and will allow parents to keep a set of school books at home. Other districts may require a deposit or charge for another set of books to cover costs. Once the books are home, it is important that they be kept *only* in the room in which homework is done. Frank has a remarkable ability to lose things. He will need supervision in holding onto the extra set of books at home. Make sure that Frank doesn't try to take those books back to school. To ensure that completed assignments and the appropriate books do get back to school, you might recommend that your child place all these materials on a table or shelf near the front door before going to bed at night. If a book bag or backpack is used to carry schoolwork, have your child put assignments and books into the bag or pack as soon as he or she is through with the work. The book bag or backpack can then be placed, in plain sight, on a table or on the floor next to the front door, to be grabbed as your child leaves for school in the morning.

We haven't forgotten Ronald. We recommend that you use for Ronald, who resists doing homework, the same procedures just outlined that you would use for Kenny, Claudia, Tracy, and Frank. You'll find additional suggestions for reducing Ronald's resistance to you and to homework in chapters 6 and 7. But first things first; we must still make sure that Ronald brings his homework home.

6

Where and When to Do Homework

Designing a Study Area

Locating and designing an appropriate study area can in and of itself lead to marked improvement in homework skills. Which room of the house or apartment should be set aside for homework? The following guidelines can be applied in a variety of different homes, although some creative problem solving may be needed when less space is available. First, you and your child should choose a room or area within a room that is relatively free of distractions. Distractions include sounds, the presence of other people, and the accessibility of activities other than schoolwork. Often we see families in which children have been encouraged to do their homework at the kitchen table. During study time, Mom is usually cooking and the other children are running in and out of the room. They may be warned by their parents not to enter the kitchen while sister or brother is doing homework, but are known to plead, "I need something that will only take a second to get . . ." They stay longer, and homework gets put aside while the older sibling complains about the disruption or starts a conversation or goes for a drink or for something to eat.

Basic Study Rules

RULE #1:   *Homework should be done in ONLY one place.*

Once a room has been designated for homework, some care should be taken in furnishing and lighting the study area. A youngster's ability to concentrate or attend to homework tasks is related to fatigue and physical comfort. Fatigue occurs more rapidly if the lighting is poor or too bright, the chair is uncomfortable, or the desk is the wrong size. Time should be given to the construction of an environment that makes studying easier.

The chair should be straight-backed and its seat at a height that permits the youngster's feet to touch the floor. Although the couch, a soft chair, or the bed may feel more comfortable, studying there may give way to napping or daydreaming. Likewise, assignments that require writing often cannot be completed legibly or neatly when the youngster works on the bed, couch, or floor. Homework must be done either at a desk or at a table. Generally, the height of the desk or table is correct when the writing surface is level with the seated child's elbows. Proper working conditions will reduce fatigue and increase the time your child is able to concentrate on studies. However, we don't expect parents to buy new desks and chairs every time the child grows. These guidelines for selecting appropriate furnishings represent the ideal. How many of us need perfect working conditions in order to do a good job? Not many. At the same time, we do not want to waste our energies fighting our environment. We want to structure an environment that helps rather than hinders the flow of homework.

Lighting should be direct; try to select a lamp that can take a 100- to 150-watt soft white light bulb. If the lighting is too dim, eye fatigue will rapidly set in and may lead to eye strain. On the other hand, bulbs brighter than 175 watts can often produce headaches from the glare. The lamp should be placed so that it does not cast shadows over the work and provides sufficient background illumination. If the work area is bright and the background is dark, fatigue often results, too, as the youngster keeps adjusting his or her eyes to the different levels of light.

The room should be designed to direct attention to the schoolwork. This means that the desk or tabletop must be free of all materials not necessary for homework. For example, a dictionary is acceptable, while yo-yos are not. Radios, comic books, magazines, model cars, hamster cages—anything that could conceivably reduce your child's attention to homework—should be removed. This also includes posters, pictures, and pennants hung on the wall directly in front of the study area. Reference material like an encyclopedia is acceptable; workbooks, rulers, and calculators can also be helpful. Many youngsters seem to spend more time looking for paper and pencils than they spend on homework. Make sure there is an ample supply of paper, pens, and pencils nearby; it also doesn't hurt to have a pencil sharpener available to handle broken points and to avoid overly smudged papers.

Suggestion #1: Limit access to your child's study area when homework is underway.

The room should be sound controlled—that is, insulated from as many outside noises as possible. The further the study area is from other household-activity centers, the better. If Marilyn practices her harp in the living room, Sam's homework should not be attempted there. If Tony loves to listen to his boom-box radio, Sam should be protected from its sound. That is, he should work in another room of the house, Tony should wear head phones, and/or radio playing should be limited to non-homework times.

The biggest source of distraction is usually the television. Therefore, homework should be done in a room as far away from the set as possible. In any case, parents should regulate the volume of the television if others are watching it while homework is being done in *another* room. Despite initial protests, it's surprising how cooperative family members become when the choice is between lowered volume and no T.V.!

There are two reasons for imposing sound-control rules in the home. An obvious one is to limit distractions. Not only does the sound interfere with homework, but when Sam hears that his favorite program is on, he will be tempted to tune his homework out and pay attention to the show. Many homework hassles revolve around the television set. The youngster hears an interesting program and wants to watch it. If he or she is allowed to start watching before homework is completed, the parents will often have a hard time later on trying to separate the youngster from the television. Often the child's answer is, "I'll get back to my homework as soon as the commercial is on." Or, "Sure, Mom. Right after this program." In either case, getting the youngster back to the homework is often an unwelcome ordeal for parents. The second reason for consistently enforced sound limits is to transmit the message that **homework is important**. In fact, homework is **very** important—more so, even, than radio or T.V! When television is allowed to disrupt homework, the message communicated to the child is that it is at *least* as important as homework.

Some youngsters, particularly teenagers, claim that they concentrate better when the radio is on. They say that having the radio on is soothing and helps them pay attention. For some youngsters this is indeed true—having the radio on does facilitate homework. Whether or not your youngster's homework performance is positively affected by the background music of a radio will have to be tested. Agree to let your son or daughter try to do the work with the music on and then review the assignments with him or her afterward. If the work is satisfactory (based on standards mutually agreed upon by you and your child), then the radio can stay on during homework time. Otherwise, permit music only after the work is completed. In the former case, make it clear that the volume cannot be set at the loud level preferred by many teenagers. There is no contradiction in avoiding the television noise and radio noise created by others while generating one's own: psychological research shows that we are more distracted by noises that we don't control than by those that we do control.

———

*Suggestion #2:   Keep noise to a minimum when home-
                  work is underway.*

In most instances, we recommend that homework
be completed in the child's bedroom. If the youngster
is used to doing homework in the family room or in
the kitchen where people are present, there is often
resistance to using the bedroom. After all, how many
of us would choose to be isolated when we have become used to being in the thick of things? Involving
your child in the decision-making process may reduce
this resistance somewhat. You can further his or her
comfortableness with working alone by first remaining in the bedroom while homework is completed and
then gradually moving yourself out of the room by
small steps. When in the room, keep conversation
with your child to a minimum. If out of the room, be
sure to praise your child afterward for working on his
or her own.

If your home has no room in which the youngster
can work alone, or if your pattern of family life pre-
cludes working alone, feel free to compromise. If the
work has to be done at the kitchen table, see if José
can do his homework when the kitchen is not needed
by everyone; that is, right after school, when snacks
are finished, maybe a quiet time in the kitchen, when
homework can be started with little outside interference, can be arranged. In contrast, the hours between
5:00 P.M. and 7:00 P.M. are often high-use times for
the kitchen. If your child chooses to study between
these hours, the kitchen is *not* the place to work. No
matter where homework is done, the activities of
other people in the home should be scheduled so that
conflicts are avoided. The family should collectively

determine homework schedules; that is, the family should meet as a group and decide who will do homework when and where. When there are two or more school-aged children in the family, a traditional way of handling the sometimes conflicting priorities of the children is to switch schedules. Therefore, if Evelyn and Ann want to do homework in the bedroom at the same time, it often helps to give Evelyn first choice on the odd-numbered months (January, March, etc.) and Ann on the even-numbered months (February, April, etc.). We recommend that whenever possible, brothers and sisters not do homework together—it's too easy for a child to start talking (or even fighting) about things other than assignments when he or she has company in the study area.

Suggestion #3: Whenever possible, have your child study alone, preferably in a bedroom.

Once selected, this study area should thereafter be the only place where homework is completed by your child. This means that your child should not do homework in the kitchen on some days and in the bedroom on other days. The goal, which is for the youngster to associate homework with a specific location in your home, is one of the first steps in developing good study habits.

Suggestion #4: Be sure the study area is well-lit, comfortably furnished, and free of non-homework materials.

Now that a study area has been choosen and stocked with school supplies, only homework should be attempted at this desk or table. If your child daydreams, that is allowed, but he or she must get up and daydream away from the desk. If your child doodles, that too is all right so long as he or she is not at the desk. These instructions may go against your present ideas about how to build study skills. The "old school" of how to develop homework habits involved designating a starting and stopping time for studying. The child would be told to sit down and start working at, say, 4:00 P.M., and would be required to remain in that seat until, say, 5:30 P.M. each day. It's not that difficult for parents to impose these time limits, but what often happens is that the child will sit at the desk and daydream throughout those ninety minutes. In other words, we can lead a child to homework, but we can't make him or her learn or complete the work. Sitting at the desk then becomes associated with daydreaming rather than with doing homework. We know that everyone's attention wanders and that people are able to concentrate for different lengths of time. Parents need to accommodate these differences, and the best way is to allow each youngster to develop his or her own homework schedule. We can't tell someone when they have reached the limit of their concentration; they will know their limit better than we do.

For example, while writing this book, each of us had periods when concentrating became difficult. When this happened, rather than sit and stare at the typewriter, a break was taken. Work was resumed when the ability to concentrate returned. People cannot be forced to pay attention. It is much more effective to design conditions conducive to the development of habits that, in turn, facilitate increased attention.

Associating a particular location with doing homework, and not diluting that association with other experiences (like daydreaming, reading novels, eating, doodling, even sleeping), will help to increase your child's attention span for homework.

Of course, the youngster should know that the amount of time spent daydreaming or doodling should be self-limiting, that he or she is expected to return to the desk as soon as attending to the work is once again possible. Many parents are reading this and saying to themselves, "My Richard would spend the next week daydreaming. This wouldn't work for him." Our experience, and that of other researchers like Israel Goldiamond, indicates that the breaks in concentration occur less frequently and for shorter periods of time the longer the child uses this approach. In the vast majority of cases we see, youngsters do not abuse the opportunity to get up from the desk. And, in fact, as we will explain later, you can provide incentives for speedy completion of the work. In a few cases, youngsters may need to be encouraged to limit their breaks to no more than five minutes.

RULE #2: Start homework at the same time every day.

Once a location is determined and the study area has been set up, the next step is to develop a homework schedule. The question is, "When should homework be done?" Once again, there is no single answer to this question. Different youngsters have different preferences. Different youngsters also have different times of peak intellectual efficiency. Some function best very early in the morning (although we very rarely recommend doing homework then) and some function best in the evening. We have no hard and fast rule for when homework should begin, only that a homework routine should be developed for the specific time that maximizes your child's willingness and ability to work. Some of the things to consider when selecting a time to start the work include (1) the preferences of your child, (2) the time it takes for your child to do homework, and (3) the work and play schedules of all people involved. For example, if your child needs supervision and you work during the day, the homework should be scheduled for the evening, when you can be present.

You may have to try out more than one schedule to find the one that works best for the child and for his or her "homework helper." The Chongs, for instance, quickly agreed on what they thought was an ideal homework routine. Their son Luke was known to be the most alert in the early evening, so it was decided that after supper he'd do his assignments. Dad worked most nights, so Mom would be the one to check Luke's work and answer questions. For the first two days of the schedule, Luke did his work whenever he wanted to and Mom did not remind him to start after dinner. Dad was getting upset; he wanted to know, "how come my wife is sabotaging the schedule?" It turned out that, while Luke was in his top form in the evening, Mom was exhausted after a long day of teaching and had little time or patience to tutor her youngest son. She preferred to work with Luke in the afternoon when she was somewhat more relaxed. Since Luke did not object to this change in study times and his work did not suffer, homework time was moved to 3:30 P.M. and family harmony was reestablished.

It is also important to keep a cushion of time when extra work is required. There are times when homework may take longer to complete; e.g., when projects are due or just before a test. The schedule should not leave homework to be done at the last minute and thus not allow for these extra-effort times. This is one of the reasons that we rarely recommend early-morning study times, even if the child wakes up at 5:30 A.M. full of energy. If the youngster cannot get the assignments done the morning that they are due, there usually won't be an opportunity later to find time to complete the work.

Meet with your child to discuss what time he or she would like to do homework. Make it clear that this is an important and binding decision. Once a time is established, that *is* the time when homework is to begin. It is *not* to be done only when and if the youngster decides that day. We are establishing habits. Habits are created by repetition, or practice. Once again, we are aware that reality may prevent perfect scheduling. There are Little League games, dentist appointments, any number of after-school activities, and all kinds of special events that interfere with a perfect schedule. These events, however, will not prevent the development of a habit of starting homework at a set time if repeated enforcement of when to begin occurs on those days with no such activities.

Most youngsters, although not all, coming home from school want a break and a snack before starting their assignments. Usually this break can last between fifteen and thirty minutes. Many students like to get homework out of the way so that they can play with their friends, and choose to do homework immediately after their snack. If your youngster decides to do that, then the rule is: "Begin homework after my snack *every* day." Although occasionally there will be conflicting activities that will delay the start of homework, this rule is to be followed with as few exceptions as possible.

Many youngsters who prefer to play with their friends or watch television when they first come home may choose to do homework before supper, say at 4:30 P.M. *Their* rule is that homework begins *every* day at 4:30 P.M. Generally, you and your child should leave enough time for the average amount of homework (one to one-and-a-half hours in elementary school and junior high, two to three hours in high school) before the supper hour. Because different families eat supper at different times, and different children have different amounts of homework and/or different rates at which they complete it, the exact starting times must be determined for each child. There is nothing wrong with wanting to play with friends first. The requirement is simply that a homework routine be established.

Many youngsters prefer doing their homework after supper. They want to squeeze all the playtime possible out of their afternoons, so they elect to postpone homework. Fine. The rule for them is: "Homework is done after supper *every* day." Our goal is to develop a habit that guides the start of homework.

RULE #3:   *Play only after homework is finished.*

After a time and place for homework have been established, it is helpful to add an incentive for completing homework quickly and accurately. It does little good if your youngster goes to his or her room, sits

For Better or For Worse. ©1984 by Universal Press Syndicate. Reprinted with Permission. All rights reserved.

at the desk for fifteen seconds, gets up to daydream for forty-two minutes, and repeats this over and over. Parents need to have gentle incentives for encouraging the timely completion of homework. These incentives usually exist already. For the youngster who chooses to do homework after school, for example, the best incentive for work completion is often the requirement that homework be done before going out to play or watching television. For teenagers, the strongest incentive may be the setting aside of time to socialize with friends via phone calls and visits. Parents should present these incentives in a positive way for them to be most effective. Listen to how different the same incentives sound depending on how they are worded: 1) *Positive*: "You can play after you finish your homework." 2) *Negative*: "You can't play until you finish your homework." The negative incentive is somewhat like a challenge. Many youngsters simply can't resist a challenge. As soon as you tell them that they *cannot* do something, they become motivated to do exactly what is forbidden. Present incentives in a positive way: "Sure, you can play with your friends as soon as you finish your homework." We have now established the basic homework rules. The details of these rules should be negotiated with your youngster and agreed upon as if they formed a contract. The rules should then be written in large letters with a magic marker on poster board or paper and placed near the desk. Here's an example of one student's chart:

JAMIE'S HOMEWORK RULES

1) Begin homework at ____ P.M. *every* day.
2) Do homework *only* at the desk (No other place).
3) *Only* do homework at the desk (Do nothing else at the desk. Daydream, doodle, etc. away from the desk)
4) Try hard . . . It's more fun!!!

That last rule that we added (number 4) may surprise parent and child. Most youngsters view homework as a chore that simply has to be done. Although there is some truth in this (i.e., the teacher expects that the work will be completed), all tasks are more fun when we try hard. When one talks to children about doing homework, one compares studying with playing basketball: "Generally one enjoys basketball more when a great effort is made, not when it is easy. Often, even when we win, we are bored unless there is a challenge to do well. Homework is really no different from other human activities in that we can have more fun when it is challenging. When we try hard to do well, we can make homework a challenge. When we simply try to get it out of the way with minimal involvement, homework is simply less fun."

Once you and your child have established these four homework rules, be prepared to praise all efforts your child makes to follow these rules. Pay attention to signs of progress and point these out to your youngster. This may mean keeping records similar to the ones you completed in Chapter 4 when asked to observe how often your child's homework problems occurred. For example, one mother jotted down when her son started homework each day. She complimented him when she noticed days when homework was started within ten minutes of the time they had agreed to earlier. It wasn't long before the boy was consistently beginning his work on time. Similarly, Sarah, remembering to do *only* homework at her desk, decided to keep track of the number of times she got up from her desk when her concentration wandered. This type of recording, called *self-monitoring*, showed Sarah that, while she was getting up ten to fifteen times each evening during the first week of following her homework rules, by the end of the second week, her concentration lapses were reduced to two or three per evening. What an improvement! When Mom and Dad were shown these records, they were quick to tell Sarah how pleased they were with her progress and encouraged her to keep up the good work. This specific use of praise and support will increase your child's ability to stick to his or her own homework routine.

Some Problem Types

While these guidelines for building solid homework routines will work for many families, there are situations that may require additional strategies for success. The following are a few of the more common problems encountered when establishing study routines with guidelines on how to handle them.

The "Don't leave me alone" child

In general, we recommend that children be encouraged to study in a quiet area away from distracting sights and sounds that interfere with completion of homework tasks. Accomplishing these goals generally means that each child will work alone, that other family members will be elsewhere in the house, out of sight. Some children, however, will be distressed by this separation, they may cry, complain, throw tantrums, or otherwise be defiant. Late afternoons and/or evenings may be the only times when their families are together, and they may not like being sent off to their rooms. If you are faced with this situation, reassure your child that you are not punishing him or her. You might find the following explanation helpful: "Children have jobs to do, and so do adults like Mom and Dad. Along with your job of going to school, you also have the responsibility of finishing homework. We know that the noise we make can make it hard for you to do your homework job well, so why not work here, where it's quiet? When you've completed your work and checked it over, we'd like you to come and talk to us [watch T.V. with us, play a game with us, etc.]."

If your youngster still protests or refuses to work apart from others, studying in the kitchen or the living room can work if the television, radio, and/or stereo remain off. You might save some paperwork from the office or household (or even read the newspaper) and work along with your child. You thereby are setting a good example and modeling desirable study behavior while also providing your child with the comfort of your presence. As discussed earlier in this chapter, you should plan gradually to "fade" yourself away from the study area. That means you will begin by sitting near your child and slowly, over a week or two, move farther from the study desk until you are outside your child's homework room. At the same time, you will want to praise your child for working alone for longer periods of time. An alternative approach, also based on this "shaping" procedure, is for the parent to tell the child, "I'd like you to try working on your own for the next five minutes [or ten, fifteen, or twenty minutes]. I'll come back then to check how your work's going." If the child continues to work alone for the specified period of time, the parent should praise him or her, then gradually set a new, and longer, time period for independent work. "That's great. You worked by yourself for five [ten, fifteen, etc.] minutes. Now let's see how much you can get done in the next ten minutes." You'll probably need to use shorter periods of time for younger children or for children who have required much one-to-one supervision, both in the classroom and at home, when completing schoolwork.

The "social butterfly" child

Here we are referring to the boy or girl whose friends tend to call frequently or drop by throughout the afternoon and evening. When the phone rings or the doorbell buzzes, off goes Linda or Bob to answer it, regardless of whether other people at home could do the same. Homework is readily put aside in favor of socializing. If these interruptions occur several times a day during study time, it's not hard to understand why homework is not completed or takes forever to get done.

Without insisting that your child become a hermit, you can suggest that socializing be limited to those times not set aside for schoolwork. For example, telephone time for calls to friends can be made conditional upon finishing homework. Or, friends can be invited over only after studying is done. That means if a phone call comes for Marie during homework time, a message can be taken and a promise to return the call given, but no other conversation should occur until the work is completed. Have your children tell their friends ahead of time about these homework schedules, and have them ask their friends to call after study times. Sometimes families can agree that during study hours, either a parent or a sibling who's already finished his or her studies will be responsible for answering the phone or door. If the sound of the telephone is just too distracting, you might consider unplugging the phone—or at least the one closest to your child's study area—until homework is over. We know of several families who decided to use their answering machines during homework hours to record all incoming calls; they programmed the machine to begin playing after the first ring so that no one would be tempted to dash for the phone. The few hours of inconvenience were well worth it in order to limit the competition for the youngster's attention and provide him or her with additional motivation to complete homework in a timely fashion.

Also included in the "social butterfly" category is the youngster who's heavily involved in after-school and evening activities. With baseball games to play, soccer practice to attend, a scouting badge to earn, and dancing lessons to take (the list could go on), this child has a hard time finding room for studying and homework in his or her daily schedule.

Achieving a *balance* between the academic and social demands made on the child's time is necessary. Otherwise, the message communicated to your boy or girl is that schoolwork and studying are unimportant compared to social activities. While it is true that these extracurricular pastimes enable a child to develop appropriate interpersonal skills and special talents, homework helps the child to develop self-discipline and the skills of self-directed study (e.g., concentrating, problem solving, conceptualizing, checking the work, etc.). It may become necessary to limit the number of outside activities in which your youngster participates. To decide if such action should be taken, have your child complete a weekly schedule of his or her activities. An hour-by-hour listing of how time was spent could be generated, or a record kept according to the types of activities the child is involved in each day. Examples of both kinds of charts follow on page 105.

If your child has less than one hour per day available for homework (*especially* if your son or daughter is in junior or senior high school), the two of you should figure out how more time can be freed for studying. Most educators agree that at least one hour per day should be available for homework when the student is in elementary school and that this time should be doubled for the high-school student. Although com-

	MONDAY	TUESDAY	WEDNESDAY	THURSDAY	FRIDAY
After-school activities and times					
Homework time					
Play time					
Supper time					
T.V. time					
Bed time					

	MONDAY	TUESDAY	WEDNESDAY	THURSDAY	FRIDAY
3:00					
3:30					
4:00					
4:30					
5:00					
5:30					
6:00					
6:30					
7:00					
7:30					
8:00					
8:30					
9:00					
9:30					

pletion of actual assignments may not take an hour or two, the child's daily schedule should be flexible enough to allow that much time without requiring late-night or early-morning studying. When more work than usual is given, or an upcoming test necessitates intensive studying, your son or daughter will appreciate having the extra time. Interestingly, some youngsters have told us that they were relieved to have to drop out of one or more activities. It seems that they were feeling pressured to excel in all they did, or to participate in activities that interested their parents but held little excitement for them.

The "Latchkey" child

This girl or boy returns home from school and spends several hours alone before a parent returns in late afternoon or early evening. This experience is common among youngsters whose mother and father both work or who are being raised in a single-parent household. In either case, this child does not have Mom or Dad around in the afternoon, either to remind him or her to begin homework or to supervise its completion. If the prime study time selected by child and parent (as discussed earlier in this chapter) is anywhere between 3:00 P.M. and 6:00 P.M., a method of signaling when to start studying will have to be developed, at least until the youngster has established a homework routine and practiced it for several weeks.

How can a child be prompted to begin schoolwork? Several parents we know use telephone calls, placed at set times during the afternoon, to remind their children when to "crack the books." This can be done directly by saying something like, "It's time to get going on your homework. What do you have to do today?" Or, and this less abrupt approach is one we prefer, a parent might say "How did your day go? Anything funny or exciting happen?" and spend a few minutes listening to the child's recollections of the day before adding, "Well, you know it's time to begin today's homework if you haven't already started. What do you plan to work on first?"

Sometimes these phone calls can deteriorate to the point where the parent nags and the child argues or rebels (e.g., hangs up). In these cases, we recommend that the student be given an alarm clock so that he or she can set the time for when studying is to begin and thereby assume more responsibility for starting the work. The youngster could set this clock in the morning, before leaving for school, or even the night before if the alarm dial has an "A.M." and "P.M." setting. As long as the child stays in the house, he or she will hear the alarm. For the student who's less likely to be at home to hear it, you might consider the purchase of a wrist watch that comes with an alarm feature. Note, however, that if there is a pattern of resistance to doing homework when parents are not around to supervise, it's simply better to shift homework time to the evening to avoid further conflict.

Time should be set aside after dinner for you to go over the work with your child. First, look for what was completed correctly and praise this effort. Next, ask your child if he or she encountered any difficulties with the assignments, and be prepared to offer help if requested. If your child says there were no problems, have him or her explain one assignment to you. Here's another opportunity to praise your child for work well done (even adolescents enjoy sharing their achievements!). This review time also enables you to pinpoint any academic weaknesses your child may be experiencing, such as difficulty reading aloud, spelling, or writing complete sentences. These deficiencies can then be brought to the attention of your child's teacher.

7

How to Do Homework

Defusing the "Homework War"

There are many ways that parents can help their children with homework as well as the development of sound study habits, time management skills, organizational strategies, and an ability to set and meet goals. While chapters 5 and 6 outlined programs that promote effective study routines, these approaches can only be used successfully when parent and child cooperate and when the bulk of homework time is not spent fighting.

One preliminary step in negotiating a truce in the "homework war" is to increase your child's motivation to tackle the assignments. Very often the mere phrase "it's time for homework" triggers arguments and tension between parents and their youngster. Because parents are older, wiser, and more mature, they must be the leaders in bringing peace to the homework war. "Children should know that they have to do homework!" "When I was a kid we did whatever our parents told us to do. Whatsamatter with kids today?" These statements may (or may not!) be true, but the attitudes they reflect are often counterproductive to resolving homework problems and to developing an alliance between parent and child. Parents must change their approach if homework is to be completed with a minimum of headaches and angry feelings.

It is very important to approach your child with no implication of blame. Although we frequently hear parents complain that children "ain't the way they used to be", we do not believe that statement is correct. Children are as they have been for thousands of years. Babies are born with exactly the same reflexes they have always had and with exactly the same needs. What *has* changed is the social situations into which they are born. In many families both parents work, and therefore operate under employment pressures in addition to domestic responsibilities. Consequently, less parental attention is given to children. Because of these increased demands on parents, it is more difficult for them to create structured routines at home; there are simply more things to be done. Children, in turn, often develop poor habits.

There is also less social structure today, and with it, less fear of authority. The authority of a teacher has diminished. Parents used to be afraid of social disapproval from a teacher if their child performed poorly and/or didn't complete assigned work. Now, with less fear, there is more permission for noncompliance, which is transmitted to the child. These social changes have created background conditions that make discipline more difficult to implement. The social changes were not created by the children.

Finally, if many parents search their memories they may recall that they too were less than perfect when *they* were children. Memory is selective, and we tend to remember those events that cast us in a favorable light. We also tend to forget incidents that caused conflict with our parents. Our parents, too, said: "Kids ain't the way they used to be . . ."

While we cannot have much effect on the social world in which we live, we can work to change specific practices of our own to establish better habits. We have found it helpful for parents to adopt a "problem-solving," not a "person-blaming," orientation. In other words, the parent must focus on what the problem *behavior*—or *behaviors*—is. The problem may be that Hank doesn't bring assignments home or that he dawdles when he should be doing his homework. This is different from the "person-blaming" approach, which might yield the response: "Hank is a lazy kid!" There is no useful future in the person-blaming orientation.

Parents must change their approach toward their child from one of anger to one of problem solving. Children cannot be blamed for having a different set of social conditions from their parents, and they cannot be blamed for not developing helpful routines. If they are blamed, they tend to rebel. Parental anger brings out defiance on the part of most youngsters, who, in turn, do what they can not to let their parents control them. Jack Brehm referred to this tendency of children to respond either to the taking away of freedoms or to the threat of their removal by an increased motivation to restore these free behaviors as *reactance*. When applied to homework, this means that if Carl believes homework is his problem and not his parents', he will directly or indirectly rebel if his parents tell him that he "must" do his homework after school. He will either directly rebel by being defiant, or he will indirectly rebel by not doing his homework or by doing it poorly. This is what we call the "push-leads-to-shove" theory. That is, when children feel pushed, they directly or indirectly shove back. These youngsters feel overly controlled, and so they resist "surrendering" to their parents. It may even be reinforcing for them to see their parents get upset. We can tell whether this is so because the frequency of their resistance increases as punishment delivered or threatened by parents increases. Parents must remove themselves from this destructive cycle by, first, calming down and, secondly, developing the problem-solving outlook that often leads to less experienced anger.

As the parent, you must talk to your youngster matter-of-factly, acknowledging that homework has become a bad experience for both of you and that you dislike being upset by homework. So, in the case of Hank previously, the parent might say, "You know, Hank, I really don't like yelling at you. Lately I've been losing my temper too quickly and that's something I want to stop."

Furthermore, the parent should communicate a belief that homework has also been an unpleasant experience for the youngster. "I guess, Hank, that you also must dislike the conflict we're having over homework. None of us seems to be getting anything out of it except hurt, angry feelings." It is often helpful for the youngster to hear that his or her parents appreciate how difficult school must be because of poor homework habits. For example, Hank's parent said:

"It must be rough on you to be in trouble with Mr. Smith at school. I know he gets mad when homework is not done."

In an overwhelming number of cases we see, youngsters welcome an opportunity to end the homework war. It is critical that parents neither say nor imply that the reason for the war is because the child is somehow deficient or to blame. It is simply a conflict into which parent and child have fallen. Bad habits on the part of both parent and child have inadvertently been created. Children as well as teenagers already know that they aren't doing themselves any favors by not completing homework satisfactorily. The last thing they want to hear is another lecture on the value of homework. They usually want an approach that helps to resolve their problems.

The next step is to develop an alliance with your youngster in dealing with the problem. "Hank, it is better for all of us if we develop a homework routine. I don't want to get so angry, and will try not to." You can then develop a climate in which Hank is able to make positive steps without feeling that he has given up rights and privileges. The key question that parents should address is, "What can I do to help?"

Off to a Good Start

Although some youngsters will arrive home from school determined to attack their homework immediately and will have energy to do so, most students require a break to relax and unwind. So, do permit some "down time" rather than pressure your child to start studying immediately. Children who are tired, hungry, anxious, or distracted by something will accomplish little no matter how hard they try. Provide a snack and allow a period for talk before homework time, decided upon by your child and you (see Chapter 6), begins. If the schedule you and your child have set up calls for after-supper homework, conversation at the table should be pleasant and should include your child.

As homework time approaches, parents may want to ask their children what homework has been assigned for that day. This would be particularly true for those parents whose children are in the early grades or are known to have trouble with organization and/or time management. A quick review of assignments can tell parent and child several things. (1) Are all necessary materials on hand? For example, will your child need to call friends for assignments? Are there supplies that must be bought for a project? Will a trip to the library be required to select a book for a book report or to look up references for a term paper? (2) How much parental assistance will be needed? For instance, is there a test to study for? Will the child want the parent to review spelling words, ask math facts, or pose questions about the social studies chapter? Has the child been assigned work covering concepts or ideas just introduced in the classroom? It's not unusual for the youngster to have more questions about such assignments or to feel less certain of his or her ability to tackle the work alone. If the child will require assistance, the parent's schedule of activities for the night should also be consulted. An 8:00 P.M. PTA meeting might mean, for example, that work needing Mom and Dad's input should be started early. (3) How much time will be required to complete homework satisfactorily before bedtime? The number of assignments and their complexity directly affect the amount of time it will take your child to do the work. Estimating this time is helpful when decisions must be reached about whether and when activities other than homework can be scheduled on any given day. For instance, if Charlene wants to watch *The Cosby Show* and *Family Ties* before her 9:00 P.M. bedtime and has math, reading, and current events assignments to do, homework should probably be started before supper so that she's finished by 8:00 P.M. Remember that the tone of these questions should be positive rather than critical; the parent's goal is to forge an alliance with his or her child. Asking "What sorts of assignments did you get today?" is okay, while commenting with "What did you forget to bring home today?" or "Let's see what I'll have to help you with tonight" is not.

Reviewing the assignments with your child also gives you opportunities to encourage your son or daughter's use of a "plan of attack" for doing homework. The plan may be as simple as deciding what assignment to do first, second, and so on. Does he or she want to start with a long, difficult assignment to get it over with, or a short, easy one? Does your child more easily make the transition to studying by beginning with "doing" work (i.e., math problems, English) or with reading assignments? Alternating between these two types of assignments often helps to maintain concentration and interest in the work. Or, the plan may involve breaking down a long-term project into smaller, more manageable tasks that can be completed over several days or weeks. For example, a book report that is due in two weeks' time might be handled with the following "plan of attack":

MONDAY:	Go to library and choose book
TUESDAY–SUNDAY:	Read 2 chapters each night
MONDAY:	Outline book report
TUESDAY:	Write first draft
WEDNESDAY:	Review and rewrite, ask Mom or Dad to read report
THURSDAY:	Type report
FRIDAY:	Turn in the report

When your child knows what is expected to be done and where to begin, he or she can approach homework with greater confidence.

Setting Realistic Homework Goals

If you plan to change the method of doing homework, you and your child will need to set agreed-upon goals. These goals may refer to how much work will be completed during a homework session, how much time will be allotted to completing part or all of an assignment, the level of accuracy to aim for, how much time the child will work without assistance, or any combination of the above. Goals serve at least four major purposes: (1) clarifying expectations for the child's performance; (2) providing incentives for "doing better"; (3) setting standards against which the child can compare his or her performance; and

(4) providing a focus for the youngster's attention that facilitates concentration.

Goals should be established through collaboration with your child rather than being forced upon him or her. Remember, you want to forge an alliance with your youngster, not foster resistance. Goals should be set only after you and your child have a clear picture of his or her current level of performance; that way, you'll be less likely to set unrealistic goals. If a goal is difficult to achieve, your child may become frustrated and discouraged. If you ask for too much, your child may choose to do nothing at all rather than to try and fail. So, start with a goal that can be readily achieved by your child rather than a goal that you think he or she "should" be able to meet. What is important is what your child *can do*, not what the child *should do*. Keep in mind the saying, "Nothing succeeds like success." When your child is able to meet a homework goal and is reinforced for this accomplishment with parental encouragement and attention, he or she will tend to try harder next time. Furthermore, as goals are successfully met, your child's sense of **self-mastery**—the confidence in one's ability to conquer obstacles and solve problems—will increase, enabling him or her to take on more difficult tasks and/or to set higher goals.

The key here is to set goals that are within the child's current skill level when some effort is exerted. In the following exercises, select the most appropriate goal for the youngsters described.

1. Your child now spells 50% of his words correctly after rehearsing for 15 minutes.

   (a) Set up a goal that specifies 100% correct after 15 minutes of study.

———

2. Your child now has to be reminded 3 to 4 times a night to start homework.

    (b) Set up a goal that specifies 70% correct after 15 minutes of study.

    (a) Set up a goal that homework will be started after 2 or 3 reminders.

    (b) Require that the child start homework without reminders from you.

3. You notice that your child leaves the study area an average of 5 times once she or he has started homework.

    (a) Tell your child that she or he can't leave the desk when it's time for homework.

    (b) Set up a goal where praise will be given for fewer than 5 breaks during study time.

Answers Below

Now consider your own child's homework performance. How long can he or she work independently before asking for help, losing concentration, or changing activities before the assignments are completed? How long does it generally take your youngster to do the work? How much of the work is completed correctly? Neatly? How many assignments are usually forgotten each day or week? For this information you may wish to return to the observations you made when pinpointing homework problems in Chapter 4. These records represent your child's current skills in completing homework and are the standards against which to design goals for his or her future performance level. Decide on realistic homework goals that you can establish with your child and write them here.

GOAL 1:   Now _____

            Next _____

            Later _____

            Final _____

GOAL 2:   Now _____

            Next _____

            Later _____

            Final _____

ANSWERS: (1) b (2) a (3) b

You'll notice that we've left space for you and your child to write in later goals, which represent the levels of performance to be worked toward once initial goals have been met, until some final level of skill is achieved. This process—called *shaping* (see Chapter 3)—of breaking down a behavior or goal into its smaller parts or steps and providing reinforcement for the attainment of each step is one of the most successful strategies known for developing complex skills such as good study habits. As your child improves at doing homework, you acknowledge and reinforce the improvement and at the same time convey the expectation that he or she will be able to do even better with time, effort, and practice.

How many steps should a goal be broken down into? Although we provided space for three subgoals and one final goal, this was an arbitrary decision. The number of subgoals that you and your child establish will depend on both how complex the behavior skill is that you wish to shape and how far your child's current performance is from the desired level of skill. For example, Mrs. Shoshinsky would like her daughter Helen to produce error-free English assignments (correct grammar and spelling). After reviewing Helen's assignments over the past two weeks, mother and daughter discover an average of ten spelling errors and three incorrect verbs (e.g., "they was" instead of "they were"). They decide that, during the next week, Helen will aim for fewer than ten spelling errors and less than three incorrect verbs per assignment. Mrs. Shoshinsky will provide encouragement throughout the week and, as a special treat, let Helen choose a movie for the family VCR on Friday night if all of the week's assignments meet or exceed the goal. As Helen's performance improved, the goal was changed to require fewer mistakes. During the second week, fewer than eight spelling errors and two incorrect verbs were expected. As the standards for her work were raised, Helen found that she took more time to look up words in the dictionary when she wasn't sure how they were spelled and began to check her assignment before handing it to her mother for review. Within six weeks' time, Helen was producing perfect papers almost every day. Since anyone can make a spelling mistake from time to time (including parents), flawless assignments were not mandatory. Here's what the chart shown on page 118 looked like after Helen and her mother had completed it:

INITIAL GOAL: 9 or fewer spelling errors, 2 or fewer incorrect verbs.

SECOND GOAL: 7 or fewer spelling errors, 1 or no incorrect verbs.

THIRD GOAL: 5 or fewer spelling errors, 1 or no incorrect verbs.

FOURTH GOAL: 2 or fewer spelling errors, all verbs correct.

FINAL GOAL: 1 or no spelling errors, all verbs correct.

Parental Attention, Approval, and Encouragement

A parent can often motivate his or her child to try to achieve homework goals by providing enjoyable, positive consequences following these behaviors. Some of the most important, readily available, and least expensive positive consequences that can strengthen homework skills are parental attention, affection, and approval. How can parents learn to use praise and encouragement effectively to foster better homework performance? It is better to make praise **descriptive** rather than judgmental or evaluative. For instance, a teenager who's been told time after time that he or she is stupid and a failure should not be expected to jump for joy when his or her parents suddenly say, "You're a bright kid!" These words, however positive, do not fit with his or her own feelings and may cause the teen to doubt the parents' sincerity or honesty. However, if this same youngster has been working hard for twenty minutes on algebra problems, he or she might believe a comment like this: "I know algebra's not one of your favorite subjects, so I can tell you've put a lot of effort into working out these problems, since you've been at it steadily. You've got all but one of them figured out correctly—that's an improvement over last week! Rechecking the calculations as you go along is really paying off for you." These words **describe** what your child did and show appreciation by the **detailed attention** you give to your child's work or behavior.

Furthermore, by praising the behavior rather than the whole child, you provide information about what constitute good study skills (in this case, effort, concentration, and rechecking the work). This **feedback** is an important learning tool for the child who's trying to figure out what homework approaches will result in satisfactory work as well as what will please you. At this stage, you will want to emphasize effort more than results. According to findings from successful treatment programs for children who were underachievers or who had specific learning problems, it is very important to give your child credit for trying and to point out to him or her how past effort has paid off in terms of improved school performance.

Likewise, it's important to be consistent with your praise and provide it frequently, especially when youngsters are developing *new* skills. Children learn new patterns of behavior best when they receive at least some recognition every time the desired action occurs. If Billy never brings all his assignments home, it will require a lot of consistent recognition from his parents to effect genuine change in this problem homework behavior. When the parent sometimes praises Billy for bringing his work home but then pays no attention on other days when the boy does this and, at still other times, nags Billy, the connection between the youngster's desirable behavior (bringing work home) and the reinforcer (attention, praise) that can strengthen it is inconsistent. Bad habits often reappear when new skills are not consistently reinforced, so we might expect that rarely will all assignments be brought home by the boy.

It may seem unnatural or awkward at first to use praise and encouragement on a regular basis, but like any new skill you learn (e.g., driving a car, learning a new sport), it takes practice and persistence to master. Find several things your child does each day to praise. Don't limit your interest and encouragement to those times when you're trying to change homework behavior. Children spontaneously help out around the house, cooperate with their siblings, share funny, warm experiences, and do many more things that bring a smile to our faces and a good feeling inside. Take time to notice those things and let your child know how proud and pleased you are—not only because you're a parent, but because they are learning and having fun. Remember, the homework war is won with love and support, not criticism or parental noninvolvement.

As your child's homework skills become more solidly developed, the detailed descriptions of what he or she has done that you liked can give way to shorter praise comments. You may also choose to use gestures, such as smiling or patting your child's back, to communicate your satisfaction and support. We've included a list of suggested words, phrases, and gestures you may feel comfortable using.

Words and Phrases

"I'm glad you're trying."	"What an improvement I can see!"
"Good thinking."	"I'll bet the teacher is pleased with how well you're working."
"You really work hard."	"Excellent."
"You're doing a good job on your own."	"Taking the time to check your work is paying off— you got them all correct."

Gestures

Smiling	Nodding your head	Ruffling child's hair
Handshake	Hugging	Kissing
Touching	Patting the back or shoulder	Arm around the shoulder

You may prefer to add some of your own phrases or gestures to this list.

Keep in mind that praise and encouragement are especially important as **feedback** (letting your youngster know how well he or she is performing) when your son or daughter is learning a new task. So, for instance, you will want to praise attempts to solve new multiplication problems more frequently than you praise the working out of simple addition and subtraction problems similar to those your child has solved in the past. As this new skill is mastered (that is, fewer mistakes are made, solutions are arrived at

For Better or For Worse. © 1984 Universal Press Syndicate. Reprinted with permission. All rights reserved.

more rapidly), you can gradually reduce the amount of praise given, but *don't* stop completely. Occasional positive attention and recognition from others is as necessary to keep good study skills going as a pay check is needed to keep people working. Without this intermittent encouragement from you for improved homework performance, your child may revert to his or her undesirable habits.

We can't stress enough the importance of paying attention to and acknowledging small improvements in your child's study behaviors. Praise and encouragement should be given for "getting better"—if you insist on perfection right from the start, you'll be disappointed and your child will become frustrated. It may help to save returned homework papers so that you and your child can actually measure the progress by comparing present work with past. That way, for example, your child can see how his or her spelling has improved or how many more fraction problems he or she can solve or how much more Spanish he or she knows than at the start of the school year.

REMEMBER: Praise and attention can be powerful reinforcers of good homework habits if you:

—ARE SPECIFIC

—ARE CONSISTENT

—ARE SINCERE

—ARE SENSITIVE TO SMALL
  IMPROVEMENTS

—PRAISE EFFORT, NOT JUST RESULTS

—PROVIDE FREQUENT POSITIVE
  ATTENTION FOR NEWLY DEVELOPING
  SKILLS

—PROVIDE INTERMITTENT OR
  OCCASIONAL POSITIVE ATTENTION
  FOR MASTERED SKILLS

Before moving on to other ways to strengthen desirable homework behaviors, let's take a moment to consider how parents inadvertently use their attention to promote children's undesirable study behaviors. It's an unfortunate reality that children tend to get noticed most when they are misbehaving rather than when they are behaving well. Parents frequently make the mistake of taking a child's good behavior for granted and forget to direct their attention and approval to the youngster when he or she is behaving appropriately. "Whew!" they may think; "Peace at last. . . . This is too good to be true. . . . Now's my chance to relax, to get the housework done, to read the newspaper. . . ." That is, if they notice the appropriate behavior at all. However, when Carrie starts to whine about how hard the work is, or Zach has to be reminded six times to start his assignments, Mom and Dad are often right there to insist that the work be done or to scold about how lazy the child is. Because attention from a parent is a reinforcer for most children, they will do the things that most often lead to this attention—including engaging in poor study habits. In a later section of this chapter, we'll talk about ways to remove your attention from inappropriate homework behaviors. Now we would like you to become more aware of the times when you provide your child with positive and negative attention during his or her homework sessions. The following exercise has been adapted from *Parents Are Teachers* by Wesley Becker (1971). We ask that you record for at least a week how often you praise and give negative feedback to your child while he or she is doing homework each day. Follow the guidelines listed here.

Steps to take:

1. DEFINE THE BEHAVIORS TO BE COUNTED.

Positive Attention: Any words or actions that communicate affection, approval, interest, or praise directed toward your child. Examples: "Good job," "That's right," "Great," "Well done," "I'm proud of you," "You really work hard," "Good thinking," "Your work is neat," a pat on the back, a hug, a broad smile, a kiss, etc.

Negative Attention: Any words or actions that communicate criticism, complaint, dissatisfaction directed toward your child. Examples: "Do it right this time," "Your work is really sloppy," "Why do you always make

so many mistakes," "Stop complaining," "Look at your paper instead of out the window," "Get back
to work," frowning, rolling your
eyes, using a sarcastic tone of
voice, etc.

2. DECIDE HOW TO COUNT THEM.

Suggestions: A. Have a paper and pencil at hand
while your child does his or her
homework and mark after P (Positive) or N (Negative) each time they
occur.

B. Have your spouse count them for
you after you have told him or her
how to record each type of attention.

3. RECORD YOUR COUNTS EACH DAY ON
THE FOLLOWING REPORT FORM.

Parental Attention

Activity: *Homework*

DATE	POSITIVES	NEGATIVES	DATE	POSITIVES	NEGATIVES
Monday			Monday		
Tuesday			Tuesday		
Wednesday			Wednesday		
Thursday			Thursday		
Friday			Friday		
Weekend			Weekend		
TOTALS			TOTALS		

Parents are often surprised to find that they are actually providing more negative than positive attention to their children during homework time. If your records indicate that this is true for you, you might wish to review this section and make a conscious effort to direct more positive attention to your child on a daily basis. It might help to continue marking down each time that approval or disapproval is communicated to your youngster so that you can monitor your improvement. With practice and effort, you're sure to see an increase in positive attention and a decrease in negative attention.

Natural Incentives

You can probably think of times when you have had to complete a necessary, but not particularly enjoyable, task. The task might have been putting up the storm windows, cleaning out the garage, preparing a presentation for work, finishing your income-tax return, or some other activity that you really didn't want to do but felt had to be done. One strategy many people use to motivate themselves at such times is to allow themselves to do something fun only after they complete the activity that isn't so much fun. We promise ourselves, "As soon as I've finished the bathroom, I'll go outside and sun myself"; "After the leaves are raked, I'll watch the football game"; or "I'll relax and go to the movies after I'm done with the report." These are all examples of the deals we strike with ourselves to accomplish jobs we might otherwise avoid or put off.

Whenever we allow ourselves to do something enjoyable in return for first doing something necessary but not as much fun, we are really applying the principle of reinforcement to our own behavior. In this case, the rewarding activity (football game, movie, sunbathing, whatever) becomes a reinforcer that increases our willingness to do the less pleasant task (the report, raking leaves, etc.). This motivation system works only if we are really prepared to follow through on our own bargain: if the leaves aren't raked, no football game is watched, or the bathroom isn't cleaned, you don't lie out in the sun. In this way, getting the reward depends on doing the less pleasant task first.

Using an enjoyable activity, privilege, or treat as a reward for following through on less enjoyable tasks is a method that also works very well with children and teenagers. It's an especially effective way of encouraging children to accept responsibilities that they presently avoid, such as starting and completing homework.

Mr. Notopoulos decided that his son, Athan, was having a hard time sticking to the homework schedule they had arranged. Homework was to be completed in Athan's room, where it was quiet and where all his school supplies were kept, but so far he hadn't sat down to work at his desk, opting instead for the floor in the living room. Mr. Notopoulos knew that his praise, attention, and recognition given when Athan went to his room to work would strengthen that behavior. But Athan never went to his room to study, so his father has had very little opportunity to praise.

How can he get Athan to start making the effort to study in his room? The first step involves thinking of things the boy really enjoys doing that can be used as reinforcers. By watching what his son chooses to do when left to his own devices, Mr. Notopoulos can find out what activities he finds pleasurable. Most children enjoy watching television, being allowed to stay up late, playing games with friends, or talking on the phone—including Athan. Any of these activities can serve as a reinforcer provided that (1) Athan enjoys the activity, (2) access to it can be made dependent upon whether Athan first does what his dad is asking of him, and (3) Mr. Notopoulos is willing to allow Athan to engage in that special activity if he completes his end of the deal by studying in his room.

Next, Mr. Notopoulos will need to set up a few rules or guidelines to establish a relationship between the enjoyable activities (the rewards) and Athan's actions that he wants to see strengthened. If watching T.V. after supper is an activity that observation has shown Athan enjoys, Dad could have a conversation with his son that sounds something like this:

"Athan, last week we sat down and figured out a plan to help you get your homework done faster and correctly. We agreed that it would be easier for you to concentrate if you worked in your room, where it's quiet and where we keep the reference books, so that you don't have to spend time looking for the dictionary or encyclopedia. So far, though, you've continued to study in the living room, and your work has taken a long time to complete and hasn't been as neat or as correct as we know it can be. From now on, homework must be done at your desk. When you study in your room, you'll get to watch T.V. and get first choice of programs that evening. Otherwise, T.V. will have to wait until the next day, and only then if you study in your room. That's our new rule: homework is done in your room, and then you can watch T.V."

If watching television is something Athan really enjoys, and if his father permits the youngster to watch television only after he has done his homework in his bedroom, a strong positive incentive for good study behavior now exists.

To teach your youngster to carry out his or her responsibilities, state that he or she must do homework before being able to do something that is more fun or receiving a special treat. For example:

"Sure, you can call your friends today. Just be sure to bring all your assignments and books home this afternoon."

"You can have a soda after you do ten math problems correctly."

"You can stay up a half an hour later tonight if your homework is done neatly and correctly by 7:30 P.M."

The next two examples are *not* examples of this activity rule. Can you figure out why they're not?

"You can play soccer after school if you'll do your homework later."

"You can go to the mall tonight if you promise to study for your test tomorrow."

The incentives mentioned above are the kinds of things that are already a part of your child's daily life. All you need to do to make them work for you is to turn them into consequences for good homework behavior. See if you can think of five or six naturally occurring positive events or treats that might encourage your child to try harder. Write them down here:

1. _____

2. _____

3. _____

4. _____

5. _____

6. _____

WARNING: Remember that for consequences to be effective, the food, activities, or privileges should only be available to the student after he or she reaches the goals the two of you have set up. Let's see what happened to Mrs. Washington, who failed to follow this rule.

Malcolm knew that he could come down for a snack only after his homework had been completed and checked by his mother. One afternoon, claiming to be hungrier than usual, Malcolm asked his mother if he could have his snack before completing his homework. A snack was a reward for homework behavior, and for the past week that had been the pattern. Mrs. Washington let Malcolm have his snack ahead of time just that afternoon. However, a few days later the same thing happened. Malcolm had an early snack and never returned to his homework. Soon, Malcolm was snacking any time, and his homework usually remained unfinished.

Through inconsistent application of the rule, both appropriate homework behavior and inappropriate behavior are rewarded, and the reward loses its effectiveness. Your youngster doesn't know when he or she will be rewarded for good study behavior or when he or she might get away with unwanted behavior. So, after you set up clear-cut, obtainable goals, decide upon a reinforcer that your child enjoys and make it available *only after* he or she achieves these goals. Tell your youngster what he or she did to earn a reward or cause the withholding of a reward.

"Your homework's finished? Great! Let's get that board game out that you and I like."

"You'll have to miss T.V. tonight because you forgot to bring your math book home today."

Ignoring

We've discussed in some detail how a parent can promote a child's good study behaviors by seeing that rewards (parental attention and recognition, enjoyable activities, etc.) immediately follow the desired homework behavior. Because a parent's attention serves as a reward or reinforcer for most children, actions that get the parent's attention will tend to be repeated in the future. We can turn this same principle around to reduce the incidence of inappropriate behavior by *removing* that attention when the child misbehaves. Withdrawing attention and approval signals to the child that he or she is acting in a way that is not appropriate. The youngster learns that he or she must behave in more desirable ways in order to gain your attention. This method of reducing inappropriate behavior through withholding attention is called *ignoring* and can be effective, if used *consistently,* in reducing or eliminating such behaviors as whines and complaints about homework, excessive requests for help, or self-critical remarks.

Let's say that your child often whines or complains about his or her homework, saying things like, "I don't want to do this. Why do I have to do this? This stuff is stupid." If you're like many parents, you might respond initially by explaining why homework is important and that it is your son or daughter's responsibility to do the work. Or, you might sympathize and sit down and go over the work in detail with your youngster. If the whining continues, as it often does, you may find yourself getting increasingly more irritated and short-tempered. Instead of responding calmly as before, you now may scold, threaten, or yell: "Shut up and just do it. . . . I don't want to hear one more complaint. . . . You keep this up and there will be no T.V. tonight." Or, you might give up and state: "All right, don't do it. We'll see what your teacher has to say tomorrow when you go in without your work." In any of these situations, your child has received a lot of your time and attention for behaving in a way that displeases you and also doesn't lead to improved homework skills. If access to you is something your child values, what do you think will happen to the frequency of whining? You're right—whining will occur more often. Certainly not what you had in mind!

How can you use ignoring to reduce whining and other annoying behaviors that interfere with homework completion? First, you'll want to inform your boy or girl that whining is something you don't like and will no longer respond to. If your child wants your attention, he or she will have to ask for it in a more appropriate way.

"When I hear whining, it makes me feel like not listening. If you want me to help with your homework, try saying in a normal tone of voice, something like, 'Mom, I'm having trouble with this. Can you help me?'"

If your child whines, remind him or her how to ask for help in a more appropriate way. If, after the reminder, your child continues to whine, ignore him or her *completely. Do not* talk or yell at your child no matter how long he or she whines. *Do not* pay attention to your boy or girl by cuddling, patting, spanking, or anything else—if possible, *do not* even look at your child. If you find it hard to resist doing any or all of these things, get up and walk away or go to another room. When you first begin to ignore, *expect* the problem behavior to occur more often or to be more intense at first. This is your child's way of determining if Mom and Dad really mean what they say. This increase in inappropriate behavior after attention or other types of reinforcement are withdrawn is technically referred to as an **extinction burst**. If you were to attend to your child at this point, after minutes of whining at possibly greater and greater intensity (louder, more insistent), you could be unwittingly *reinforcing* or rewarding him or her for this increased whining! What your child would learn is that the way to get Mom or Dad's attention is to whine even longer and louder. So, if you choose to ignore certain unwanted homework behaviors, *be consistent*—ignore the behavior for as long as it lasts.

Ignoring *only* works when you combine withdrawal of attention for inappropriate behavior with the giving of attention for desirable behavior. This means that when your child speaks to you without whining, you must be quick to tell the child that you like it when he or she talks to you this way, in a normal tone of voice. Or, when your child stops asking over and over again for help and starts to complete the work on his or her own, tell your youngster that you're pleased to see him or her attempt the assignment first alone and that you'll be there to help or check the work a little later. In a sense, you're helping your child to *replace* inappropriate behaviors, not just *erase* them. You're teaching your child which behaviors will earn your time and attention, and which ones won't.

Likewise, ignoring provides parents with an alternative to using more aversive punishments such as yelling, making critical remarks about the child, or slapping the child. These stronger forms of punishment often produce unwanted side effects such as an increase in the child's resistance to parental direction and a decrease in the parent's ability to focus on positive behaviors displayed by the child. In short, these procedures do nothing to reduce tension or conflict between parent and child, and usually increase bad feelings.

Ignoring also gives parents a way to respond to homework behaviors that irk them but do not interfere with their youngster's ability to complete the work adequately. Here we refer to the times when your child fidgets in his or her seat, rocks back and forth, taps or twirls his or her pencil, fiddles with papers and pages, hums, or gets in and out of the seat as concentration is developed (see Homework Rule 3 in Chapter 6), but still manages to get the work done. Realize that these fidgety behaviors are bothersome to *you*, not to your child. Resist the temptation to scold your child for these actions; practice ignoring them. Otherwise, you unknowingly can interfere with and disrupt your child's studying, which may lead to more serious homework difficulties later.

What behaviors does your child engage in that you think you could ignore? List them below *and* write down an alternative positive behavior that you *would* pay attention to. An example is provided for you.

I COULD IGNORE: INSTEAD I'D REINFORCE:

1) *my third-grader's count-*   1) *his attempts to solve*
   ing on his fingers to   *math problems with*
   solve a problem   *paper and pencil*

2) _____   2) _____

   _____   _____

   _____   _____

3) _____   3) _____

   _____   _____

   _____   _____

Parents as Homework Consultants

Most parents and teachers consider a major goal of homework to be the development of an ability to complete independent work. Independent study habits are rarely developed when the parent constantly stands over the child during homework. Nor does a child learn to be self-reliant if a parent is always quick to provide help and, more specifically, gives answers to assignments without first encouraging the child to solve the problems.

Following the recommendations of clinical psychologist William Stixrud, we suggest that you adopt the role of "homework consultant," particularly as your child grows older and can reasonably be expected to have mastered many of the academic skills upon which his or her homework is based. According to Dr. Stixrud, as a "consultant" you may wish to put time limits on your involvement. For example, you might indicate that you will be available to help between 7:00 and 8:00 every weeknight. Then be available to help in a friendly, supportive manner. Choosing an hour a little later in the evening should give your boy or girl sufficient time to try to work out the assignments alone before coming to you. Work "overtime" only as a reward to your child for good effort, never for lack of effort. That is, agree to review homework and provide additional assistance past 8:00 P.M. (or whatever time you set for the end of your consulting period) if your child demonstrates that he or she attempted to complete the work to the best of his or her ability but hasn't been entirely successful.

Dr. Stixrud points out that at the start of your appointed "homework consulting" hour you may ask if your child would like help. If the answer is "no," refrain from badgering, threatening, scolding, or extensive questioning about assignments. This is hard for many parents but worth the effort in the long run. If your child turns down assistance but then panics at bedtime because the work is not finished, be firm. It is now bedtime and your child needs rest. If he or she chooses to work early in the morning to finish, that decision is up to him or her—your helping time is from 7:00 to 8:00 (or whenever) in the evening. A child who doesn't finish homework will have to face the consequences at school. You must not try to protect your child from the natural consequences of irresponsibility; however, be available for help, as before, the next day during your established "consulting hour." It has been our experience, as well as Dr. Stixrud's, that children will rarely spend more than a few days testing whether you mean business with your limits on helping with homework. They will ask for or accept your help so long as it is not forced on them.

Self-Instruction Training

Parent homework consultants are sometimes asked for specific answers to assignments. This may reflect the child's real difficulty in understanding how to approach the work. At times like these, you may wish to give suggestions as to the steps he or she should follow to obtain a correct answer. For example, you might work a math problem out loud—talking yourself through the solution step by step (see the inset), reminding yourself to check your work, and praising yourself for reaching the correct answer. Then have your child work through the next problem or problems; you provide the instructional questions and encourage him or her to respond with the appropriate verbal solutions, as shown in the sample parent-child exchange. Finally, have your child complete several problems independently using this "talk-it-out" method; be sure to praise his or her efforts! Encourage your youngster to ask him or herself these questions when faced with particularly troublesome problems before coming to you for help.

Problem

$$\begin{array}{r} 33 \\ +18 \\ \hline \end{array}$$

1) What is it I have to do?
   I have to add 33 and 18.

$$\begin{array}{r} {\scriptstyle 1} \\ 33 \\ +18 \\ \hline 1 \end{array}$$

2) What's the first thing I need
   to do? I need to add the 3
   and the 8 in the "ones" column.
   3 plus 8 equals 11, so I have
   to put a 1 in the "ones" column
   in the answer and then carry a
   10 over to the "tens" column.
   I'll put a 1 above the 3 in the
   "tens" column to remind me that
   I have to add an extra 10.

$$\begin{array}{r} {\scriptstyle 1} \\ 33 \\ +18 \\ \hline 51 \end{array}$$

3) What do I do next? Well, I have
   to add the 1, 3, and 1 together
   in the "tens" column. I get a
   5 there, which is the same as 50.

4) Am I finished? Yes. My answer is
   51.

$$\begin{array}{r} 51 \\ -33 \\ \hline +18 \end{array}$$

5) How do I know if my answer's right?
   I can re-check my arithmetic to see if
   33 + 18 equals 51—and it does! I can
   also subtract 33 from 51. It equals 18.
   That is proof the answer is correct.

6) How'd I do? Good for me—I got it
   right!

Problem	Parent says:	Child responds:
1½ hours = ___ minutes	1) What is it I have to do here?	1) I have to figure out how many minutes make 1½ hours.
	2) What's the first thing I need to do?	2) I have to change 1½ hours into minutes. There's 60 minutes in one hour. That's part of the answer.
	3) What do I do next?	3) Now I still have to figure out how many minutes make half an hour. That would be the same as half of 60, or 30 minutes.
	4) Am I finished?	4) No, now I have to add 60 minutes and 30 minutes. 60 minutes plus 30 minutes equals 90 minutes.

Problem	Parent says:	Child responds:
	5) *How do I know if my answer's right?*	5) *Let me check my math. 2 divided into 60 is 30. 30 plus 60 is:*
		0 + 0 is 0 in the "ones" place. 6 + 3 is 9 in the "tens" place. The answer is 90 minutes.
	6) How'd I do?	6) Good for me. I got it right!

Problem

Use each spelling word in a sentence. The first word is "'brief.'" Child asks instructional questions and then answers them:

1) *What is it I have to do?* I have to make up a sentence using each of my spelling words.

2) *What's the first thing I need to do?* Find out what word to use in the first sentence. It's "brief." Maybe I'd also better know what it means.

3) *If I'm not sure what "brief" means, how can I figure it out?* Ask Mom or Dad—or look it up in the dictionary! I look up the word, "b-r-i-e-f." There, I found it. It means "using a few words or taking a short period of time."

4) *Am I finished?* No, I have to use "brief" in a sentence. Let's see, how about, "I wrote a *brief* note to my friend"?

5) *How do I know if my sentence is okay?* I check to see if I have all the capital letters I need—yes. Did I put the right punctuation mark at the end? Yes—a period. Does my spelling look correct? Yep. Do I have a noun and a verb in my sentence? Sure do.

6) *How'd I do?* Pretty good—the sentence looks and sounds all right. Let's do the next one.

This method is called *self-instruction* because the child learns to teach him or herself the best way to approach and solve a problem. Self-instruction helps to slow down the child who otherwise rushes through his or her assignment, making careless mistakes and/ or producing sloppy work. It is particularly effective when taught to youngsters in the early grades of elementary school.

As your child grows older, this self-instruction approach becomes the basis of a more involved self-directed method for tackling assignments like answering questions at the end of history or science chapters or solving algebra or geometry problems. This form of self-instruction, sometimes also called **problem solving**, enables the older child or teenager to break a problem down into its smaller steps that must be completed in order. Direct your older child to Chapter 8, where he or she will find a series of questions to guide older students who may be stumped by a homework task.

8

Projects, Papers, and Taking Tests
(Tips for the Older Student)

Projects and Papers

You've probably noticed that as you've gotten older, the type of homework assigned has changed. No longer are you expected just to complete math dittos or study your spelling words for Friday's test. More often than not, you are given assignments that require more than overnight preparation; for example, book reports, term papers, and science projects. When undertaking such an assignment, you'll need to do some rebudgeting of your normal study time over a period of several days to several weeks so that you can complete the report or project in gradual steps. Putting off one of these major projects until the night before it's due *does not* work. If you do put it off, you and your family will be frustrated, you'll be anxious and required to "burn the midnight oil" in order to get it finished on time, and you'll feel grouchy and dissatisfied with your completed project.

We find that this "I-don't-get-to-work-until-it's-too-late" problem usually occurs because the student is overwhelmed or scared by a task he or she isn't certain how to handle or complete. In this section, we'll show you step by step how to plan for and carry out projects—in short, we will provide you with a "plan of attack" for mastering long-term assignments. The following is an outline of the plan; each step will be described in detail.

PLAN OF ATTACK

(1) Define your goal in general terms.

(2) Figure out what information is needed and available— revise your goal if necessary.

(3) Develop an outline.

(4) Construct a timetable for assignment completion.

(5) Identify people who can be used as resources. Where can you go for help?

Defining Your Goal

What assignment has been given? What are you expected to do? Sometimes the teacher will assign a specific topic or tell you exactly what she or he wants you to do. But, more often, the teacher only suggests a general area and the student is left to pick his or her own topic within that area. If you have a choice of topics, we first recommend that you choose one that is interesting and enjoyable for you. Work is done more readily and is more thoroughly completed when the student is excited by the subject area.

Figuring Out What Information is Needed and Available

At the same point, recognize that the topic of your project will also be influenced by the amount of information available on this subject as well as by any requirements from your teacher concerning reference materials. For example, you may want to do a report on "crack", an illegal drug whose use has reportedly grown to epidemic proportions even though it has only recently appeared. However, your teacher may want you to include books in your bibliography, in addition to magazine articles and newspaper features. You'll probably find that no books have yet been published on this drug, and thus may have to choose another topic.

Therefore, the first step in picking the right topic is a *quick overview of the field*. You need to know how much reference material is available on a topic before you commit yourself to it. Reference librarians indicate that this is the major problem encountered by students: selecting topics that have either too much or too little information available. In the first situation, the student will have to work to narrow down his or her topic; in the second case, the student will probably want to pick a related topic on which more has been written.

Where should you start when conducting this overview? Encyclopedia articles are excellent first choices for several reasons. They're brief, generally written by authorities in the field, often suggest other, more specific subjects included under their general area, and provide references where more information can be found. If the subject is something current, you may not be able to find an encyclopedia article on it. In that case, librarians will recommend that you try the *Reader's Guide to Periodical Literature* and *The New York Times Index* (ask the librarian how to use these reference materials). These indexes will direct you to any recent magazine and newspaper articles that have appeared on your topic of interest. Conducting such an overview will allow you to ask yourself, "What aspect of this area sounds as though it would make an interesting paper or presentation?"

Although you should not rush into the specific topic of your paper or project, it should be chosen reasonably quickly. Dr. Marvin Cohn, a noted educator, suggests that the hunt for a topic should take no more than 10 percent of the total time available for the project. So, if you have four weeks to complete a report, plan to spend no more than three to four days in selecting your topic.

Once you have a topic, you need three other things: (a) a bibliography or list of information sources for your paper; (b) a body of information about the topic you've chosen; and (c) an outline or tentative plan of subtopics you plan to discuss in your paper.

The bibliography serves two purposes. It begins as a list of books and articles that may contain useful information for your paper. We strongly recommend that you list on separate three-by-five-inch index cards each book or article you consult. Each card should contain the author's full name (last name first), the title of the book, the name of the publisher, publication. For a magazine or newspaper article, you should write the author's full name (last name first), the title of the article in quotes, the name of the magazine or newspaper, its date of publication, its issue number, and the page numbers of the article. As you read each reference, you can then mark its accompanying card as being "useful" or "not useful." These notations will be helpful when you organize information for the writing of the paper.

Putting each reference on a separate index card also makes the task of arranging your bibliography in alphabetical order an easy one. All you need to do is rearrange the cards by the author's last name. Cards can be added without rewriting your list which would be required if references had been written alphabetically on sheets of paper.

Developing an Outline

In his book *Helping Your Teenage Student* (E.P. Dutton: 1979), Dr. Marvin Cohn writes that a good outline should have the following characteristics:

CHARACTERISTICS OF A GOOD OUTLINE

I. It must be relatively brief.
   A. The outline should use abbreviations and meaningful phrases instead of longer sentences.
   B. Some of the details and examples mentioned in the text must be dropped.
II. The outline should clearly show the framework of ideas contained in the material the student has read.
   A. The title should clearly state the main topic so that the reader knows what he or she will be learning about.

    B. The outline should clearly show that the main topic is divided into a number of subtopics or main ideas. These subtopics are:
        1. Each of about equal importance.
        2. Of less importance than the main topic, since each subtopic is only a part of it.
    C. If necessary, each subtopic should be clearly supported by details that, in turn, are:
        1. Each of about equal importance.
        2. Of less importance than the subtopic, since each detail is only part of it.

(adapted from pages 193–194)

Each idea's position on the page shows its importance. The main topic, the most important idea in the outline, is indicated by the title. The title's importance is shown by the fact that each of its words starts with a capital letter and that it is the statement that comes first, before all others. The importance of the remaining ideas of the outline is shown by their distance from the left-hand margin. The closer the idea is to the margin, the more important it is. All subtopics or main ideas start at the margin and are marked or set off by Roman numerals (I, II, III, and so on). The more important details used to support them should start about an inch further right. Each important detail supporting a main idea is preceded by a capital letter, starting with **A**. Less important details should start still another inch farther to the right and are marked with Arabic numbers (1, 2, 3, and so on).

Your outline is the blueprint or plan for your paper or project. Here's another example of an outline—this is one we used when writing the sixth chapter of this book.

WHERE AND WHEN TO DO HOMEWORK

I. Characteristics of a good study area
    A. Quiet
    B. Free of distractions
    C. Well-lit
    D. Appropriate furnishings
    E. Readily available study materials

II. Selecting a time to do homework
    A. Consider child's schedule of activities
    B. Consider parent's schedule of activities
    C. Room for change/flexibility

III. Your child's homework routine
    A. The four homework rules
    B. Developing the association between time, place, and studying
    C. Rewarding your child's use of the routine

IV. Overcoming common problems with the homework routine
    A. The child who doesn't want to work alone
    B. The "social butterfly" child
    C. The child whose parents work

V. Charting progress

Even when a formal paper or report is not the final goal, outlines can be useful for organizing and planning the steps you need to follow in order to complete, for example, a science project. Here's an outline we remember using in biology class when we had to grow bacteria under four different conditions in order to determine the best environment for its growth.

I. Materials needed
    A. Petrie dishes
    B. Agar (seaweed broth)
    C. Cotton swabs
    D. Source of bacteria

E. Lamps
F. Heat source
G. Thermometer
II. Growing conditions
    A. Light + Heat
    B. Light + Room temperature
    C. Dark + Heat
    D. Dark + Room temperature

Developing a Timetable

In order to finish your project and feel good about the work you've done, it's important to map out each step you must complete and the period of time you believe is reasonable in order to complete each step. Some students use their monthly calendars for this purpose and mark in large, colored letters the day when the assignment is due. As they complete each phase of an assignment, they indicate their achievements on the calendar so that they have a record of their steady progress toward the goal. We recommend that you work out a timetable for completing projects, much like the schedule we later suggest you develop when preparing for exams. For example, if a book report is due in two-and-a-half weeks, your timetable for its completion might look like that at top of page 152.

Always leave a "margin of error" when constructing your timetable—that is, always expect the unexpected and leave enough time to complete stages of your project even if you're faced with a delay or a change in plans. For example, if your history report will require you to ask for books through interlibrary loan, be sure to budget the two to three weeks it will probably take for those materials to arrive.

	SUNDAY	MONDAY	TUESDAY	WEDNESDAY	THURSDAY	FRIDAY	SATURDAY
WEEK 1		Report given	Go to library Select book	Select book today Read Ch. 1 & 2	Read Ch. 3 & 4	Read Ch. 5 & 6	Read Ch. 7 & 8
WEEK 2	Read Ch. 9 & 10	Work on outline		Write rough draft Have parents review			Write 2nd draft
WEEK 3	Finish 2nd draft Parents review	Type final draft & review		Turn in report			

Identifying People as Resources: To Whom Can You Go for Help?

When problems or questions arise as students work on projects or papers, they typically rely on their parents or teachers for help. If you're stumped, for example, when it comes to writing your outline or composing paragraphs that help the flow of ideas in your paper, we, too, recommend that you consult with your parents and teacher(s). But we also strongly suggest that you seek out the librarian at your school or community library. These professionals can be some of the most helpful people to query when you've been assigned to complete a project, write a report, or prepare a presentation for class. Unfortunately, many students have developed faulty attitudes about librarians that can keep them from seeking this assistance. For example, some youngsters think that the librarian can show them where to find a good book to read, but would not know where to get information on buried treasure in the South Pacific. Wrong! Or, they think that librarians don't want students to ask them questions because they're too busy reshelving books or telling other youngsters to be quiet. Truth of the matter is, most librarians are thinking, "Ask me, ask me, ask me! If only someone would ask me a question!" They've studied for many years to provide students and the general community with assistance in answering research questions.

What kinds of help can a librarian provide? We talked to two librarians: Louise Miller, M.L.S., a school librarian for Clinton Township, New Jersey; and Marilyn Levine, M.A., a former reference librarian at Suffolk County Community College in New York. According to their report, the school or reference librarian can teach you how to capitalize on the numerous sources of information available to you in the library. She or he can show you how to use the library's four major reference areas, which include:

1) the card catalog
2) the reference section—where you can find specialized encyclopedias that give more in-depth information on topics ranging from baseball and comic books to science and technology
3) the *Readers Guide to Periodical Literature* and *The New York Times Index*
4) the vertical files—which contain government pamphlets and documents and are ordered by subject or topic

[*Note*: Some libraries may also have community resource files that contain information about local organizations and businesses]

So, for example, the student who wished to learn more about "crack" or, another controversial issue, the death penalty for juveniles would be directed to the *Reader's Guide* and *The New York Times Index* to locate current magazine and newspaper articles on these topics. Another student who is looking for information on the U.S. space program would be directed to books and to the vertical file, where he or she could find NASA documents detailing what astronauts eat when they're in space and even how they go to the bathroom! Or, the youngster who needs information about government officials would be introduced to the reference section, where he or she could look in an almanac for current salaries of Supreme Court Justices and the President. You may also be surprised to find that your library is equipped to lend you filmstrips, assist you in creating transparencies for the overhead projector you're supposed to use in your presentation, and provide video equipment for your use if you decide to do a film project!

Preparing For and Taking Tests

The most effective preparation for quizzes, tests, and final exams begins days and weeks before the actual test is given. This preparation involves regular classroom attendance, timely completion of all homework assignments and readings, active review of course material from the second day of class onward, and more intensive studying beginning at least four to five days, and ideally two weeks, before the scheduled test. The fact is, the more time you spend on a subject, the more knowledge you will retain, the more confident you will feel about your ability to handle test questions adequately, and the less anxious you will be before and during the examination. Let's look at this preparation process in greater detail.

1) *Classroom preparation:* Be sure to attend class regularly and to listen actively to what is said during each session. Sometimes it's hard to pay attention to what the teacher is saying if you're sitting near the doorway or windows, near the back of the room, or next to classmates who like to talk a lot. Whenever possible, we recommend that you sit near the front of the classroom, where you will be less distracted by the sights and sounds of those around you and where the teacher's nearness (and his or her ability to catch you "napping," daydreaming, or socializing with others) will increase the likelihood that you will pay attention during the lesson.

Come to class prepared. That is, come with notebook and pens or pencils to jot down notes, ideas, formulas, equations, and definitions covered in the class discussion. If you have a few moments before class begins, take that time to review quickly your notes from your last class and to look over your assignment. This activity "primes" your mind for the lesson about to follow. It increases your ability to identify the key points made during the class as well as the chances that you will feel confident enough to participate in classroom discussion (and we all know that teachers recognize and appreciate participation by interested and well-prepared students!).

2) *Taking notes:* Even with the best of memories, it's impossible for anyone to remember everything he or she hears in class; nor is it necessary to try to remember everything. Students should learn how to

select the important information presented in their teachers' day-to-day lessons so that their preparation for exams can be efficient and effective. While most teachers will review material covered in class textbooks, it is a rare teacher who relies entirely on this information for lesson planning. Even when class lectures are primarily a rehash of information covered in the book, the information that is presented can be judged to be the most important from the teacher's point of view, and thus the most likely to be asked for on quizzes and tests. Therefore, it's to the student's advantage to learn how to take effective notes in class.

Should you try to write down every word? No. Not only is such a task generally impossible, but providing a word-by-word transcript of the lesson fails to help you identify the most important points, as they get lost amid the details. One note-taking method that has been recommended time and again is to use eight-and-a-half-by-eleven-inch sheets of looseleaf notebook paper. Draw a vertical line about one-third of the way in from the left edge of each sheet of paper. This column is later used for key words and phrases from the notes. During class, write your notes on the right-hand side of the page. Notes should contain only important information that supports or explains the main points of the lesson. Abbreviations are fine as long as you can later understand what they mean. Most of all, write your notes as legibly as possible; they'll be no help to you later if you can't read them. When you get to the end of one idea, skip a few lines before starting the next one. Leave blank space so that you can add other material later.

You may ask, "What is important to write down?" Fortunately, teachers provide clues as to what is important. Listen closely at the beginning of the class, because the teacher will say, "Today I'm going to cover. . . ." or "Today we'll look at. . . ." or "Today's topic will be. . . ." In other words, this is the "theme" or objective of the class; be sure to get it in your notes.

A teacher's tone of voice often gives clues as to what is important. For instance, the teacher may slow down to state something clearly and precisely when it is important and should be remembered. He or she may use phrases such as "The purpose of. . . ." or "Three reasons for. . . ." or "In summary. . . ." to signal the class that important information is about to be presented. What the teacher spends a lot of time on is also important information, especially if he or she repeats certain facts or points. Certainly, what a teacher writes down on the board is worth taking down in your notes. Finally, if you have any doubts about what is important material, ask your teacher.

Note Taking Example

MAIN TOPICS	PROBLEMS WITHIN THE[1] ROMAN EMPIRE
	Following the Punic Wars, fighting broke out within Italy be-
Populares versus the Optimates	tween the *Populares*, who were mostly poor farmers, soldiers,

[1] These notes are based on material appearing in *Our Common Heritage: A World History* (pp. 110-112), Lexington, MA: Ginn and Company, a high-school textbook written by Daniel Roselle (1981).

MAIN TOPICS

PROBLEMS WITHIN THE[1] ROMAN EMPIRE

and city workers, and the *Optimates*, who were the wealthy merchants and businessmen.

The Populares had lost their property during the war and often couldn't find work even though they had fought for their country in the war. Many of the Optimates became rich during the war by trading. Some bought up the farms of the Populares. Many were Senators. In general, the Optimates were not concerned with the plight of the Populares.

Heroes of the Populares: The Gracchi Brothers

Two brothers, Tiberius and Gaius Gracchus, supported the cause of the Populares. Each was killed because of this. Tiberius, when elected Tribune, tried to limit the size of the farms a person could own. Gaius later asked that grain be sold at low prices to the poor and that unemployed Romans be allowed to settle in the Empire's colonies. Both tried to use their influence in ways that angered the Senators and led to their deaths.

Civil war: Marius Loses to Sulla

Populares backed *Marius*, a general who was elected a Consul in 108 B.C. Even though he and his army lost to that of *Sulla*, who was backed by the Senators and Optimates, he made changes in the Roman army that were long lasting. Instead of a draft, people volunteered to become soldiers and often became professional soldiers. They were more loyal to their generals than to government officials. In later years, military strength often decided who would rule the Empire.

You should read your notes over again *as soon as you can after the class* (e.g., in study hall or at home at night). This review is critical to the process of helping you learn and remember what is covered in class each day. Reviewing your class notes promptly also allows you to complete or write out more clearly any incomplete or confusing notes while the information is still fresh in your mind. At this time you can use the left column to jot down a word or phrase that represents the major divisions or subsections of your notes. These phrases will later become headings to help you locate specific sections of your notes for review, and can also be turned into questions for self-testing as you prepare for an upcoming quiz or exam (more on this later).

3) *Study strategies*: Besides setting up a homework routine so that you have a regular time and place to do your work, the way in which you study or review your textbooks and class notes can have an important impact on how well you do on your exams. Over the years, educators and researchers have developed and recommended a variety of approaches for studying.

These methods all have the major goals of strengthening your ability to extract meaningful information from what you read and to recall it accurately. The study method most frequently recommended is one developed by Dr. Frank Robinson (1946, 1971) and is known as the SQ3R method (Survey, Question, Read, Recite, Review). SQ3R is a powerful tool for students because it incorporates much of what we know scientifically about how people learn and remember. As is the case with most new and useful strategies, it isn't applied as effectively or as quickly the first few times you try it, but with repeated practice, we think you'll find that your studying goes faster and your test grades improve! The five steps to this approach are described next.

STEP 1: Survey or preview the material.

At this stage, your goal is to get a quick overview of the information that is covered in your chapter. You want to get a general idea of what you're going to be learning. Being familiar with the material helps you to understand it better. Most textbooks are organized and written in ways that will help you to identify the major points of each unit. Read the questions at the end of the chapter first. Then read the introductory paragraph, the **boldface type** used for headings and subheadings, and the summary paragraph at the end of the assignment. Or, you might choose to read the topic sentence (usually the first or second sentence) in each paragraph in order to get a general idea of what is covered. Be sure to look at the pictures and read the captions beneath them. Read over all maps, charts, and graphs in the chapter.

*STEP 2: Ask yourself questions about
the material you're about to read.*

For this purpose, you might use the questions at the end of the chapter, questions your teacher has distributed, or questions of your own. You can do this easily by turning the chapter's headings and subheadings into questions. For example, if your heading is "The Scientific Method," your question might be "What is the scientific method?" or "What is the importance of the scientific method?" Ask yourself what will be the important information contained in the assignment. Questioning also helps you to connect the information in the assignment to what you already know.

STEP 3: Read the assignment.

Read carefully but quickly—you're reading for ideas *and* answers to the questions you've posed. Your preview of the written material will have started you thinking about the topic you're studying and will put the major areas of discussion in your mind, increasing your ability to sort out information and make sense of it. If the book is yours, underline the important sections and make notes about the material in the margin. If the book belongs to the school, make notes in your notebook (see earlier section on note taking). *Caution*: Be selective both in note taking and in underlining. Nonspecific note taking takes up too much time and is useless because it doesn't help you to organize your notes or your thinking. Too much underlining also does nothing to help you identify the key points and the *most* important information in your textbook chapters. You end up having to re-read the entire unit rather than skim over its high-lights or critical ideas.

STEP 4: Recite the material.

Remember, understanding what you read is not enough. You must imprint the material in your mind so that you can remember it when you're tested. Here are three methods students have found useful:

a) Write summaries in your notes of the material to be remembered. Putting the information into your own words and writing it down are effective memory aids.
b) State your questions and answers out loud. Rehearsing the material by saying and hearing it will greatly im-prove your memory of it.
c) Try to relate the material you've learned to other experi-ences or other information. For example, when study-ing the Constitution, you might ask yourself, "How does the Bill of Rights affect us right now?" Or, when review-ing physics laws and formulas, you might consider, "What would happen if the Law of Gravity had not been discovered?"

STEP 5: Review the material.

Reflect upon what you've read. What were the main ideas? Go over your notes and skim what you've read for a few minutes at least once or twice a week.

Preparing For the Exam

When actually starting to review for a test, *begin early.* For a final examination, this means from two to three weeks in advance; for a unit test, start at least one week ahead. A quiz probably requires two to three days' review. Why is it important to start your review early? You gain a psychological advantage by preparing in advance—you'll feel that you, not the test, are in command. Secondly, it takes time to carry out the repeated review of course information that is essential to the learning and recalling process. Five one-hour review periods spread out over five days are far more helpful than seven hours of attempted study the night before the exam. Cramming tends to increase your anxiety, which, in turn, usually interferes with your ability to study. Cramming everything into your head in one session *doesn't* work: what information does get in is quickly lost, sometimes before the test is over, and is rarely well integrated with what you learned earlier in the marking period.

Just as families are asked to develop schedules for when and where homework is to be completed, stu-

Midway through the exam, Allen pulls out a bigger brain.

The Far Side. © 1986 by Universal Press Syndicate. Reprinted with permission. All rights reserved.

dents often find it useful to draw up a study schedule to help them plan their review sessions before a test. We've included a sample review-schedule that is adapted from a student study-guide distributed by one Long Island high school (Smithtown Central School District, 1984, page 8).

FINAL EXAM STUDY SCHEDULE

	SUNDAY	MONDAY	TUESDAY	WEDNESDAY	THURSDAY	FRIDAY	SATURDAY
WEEK 1			Test announ-ced		Plan re-view schedule		
WEEK 2	Review #1	Discuss ?s with teacher		Review #2			Review #3
WEEK 3		Review #4		Final Review	TEST		

During each of these review sessions you'll want to do the following:

(1) Gather all of your materials: books, notes from class, and past exams from the class.

(2) Identify your trouble spots. Go over these again carefully; one student told us that she would look for other textbooks to read when she had trouble understanding a certain subject as it was presented in her book. If some points are still unclear, speak to your teacher about them; now is the time to ask questions. If you're a little nervous about asking for help, imagine the payoffs. For just a few minutes of feeling uncomfortable, you'll get in return the understanding and confidence necessary in order to do well on the test. Isn't the discomfort worth it?

(3) Budget your time so that you'll spend the greatest amount on the hardest or most complex topics.

(4) Review your notes and handouts from class—check over assignments you've completed since the last test. Try to predict the exam questions. What has the teacher stressed in class? What appear to be the most important topics emphasized in your readings and class notes? Think how you would answer each question, then write your answers. This is a particularly useful exercise when you're about to take an essay test, since it gives you practice in organizing your ideas and supporting details. After you've written a sample response, check that you've started with a relevant topic statement, provided evidence to support your ideas, and ended with a summary or conclusion that clearly follows from the content of your essay answer.

(5) The night before the exam, go through all your materials one last time. Get a good night's sleep so that you can awake rested and ready to tackle the test. Many people feel better if they have a meal before taking tests; if this is true for you, plan enough time to have breakfast.

(6) Take everything you'll need for the exam—soft-lead pencils, pens, erasers, a calculator, paper—with you to the classroom. Arrive in class either on time or a little early so that you have time to settle yourself and get comfortable before the test begins. Some students, to make sure that they get to all questions before time is up, bring a large-face watch to help them pace themselves as they move through the test.

Your teacher has just entered the classroom and tells you to put all notebooks and papers away. It's time for the exam! It's your chance to show your teacher how much you've learned through your conscientious attendance in class, completion of assignments and readings, and extensive review. In order to guarantee that your advance preparation will not have been in vain once the exam is passed out and you are told to "Begin," do keep in mind the following suggestions as you take the test.

Test Taking Tips

*Read all directions carefully
before answering questions.*

One of the most common causes of poor test performance is failure to follow directions. Before choosing your answer, read carefully the instructions for each section and read each question thoroughly to make sure that you understand what is wanted. If the instructions aren't clear to you, now is the time to ask the teacher for clarification. Be sure that you understand how to complete answer sheets. For example, some teachers now may give exams that are scored by an OpScan, a machine that's preprogrammed to score exams by mechanically scanning the answer sheet and automatically marking incorrect answers. For the machine to differentiate accurately between correct and incorrect answers, the student usually must mark the form with a No. 2 lead pencil and make no more than one mark per question on the answer sheet.

Remember to erase all stray marks, especially if you've marked items for return or changed an answer. Check to see that all answers have been recorded in the correct space and that each question has only one answer.

Use time wisely.

Poor use of time during the test frequently results in students failing to finish the exam or rushing through it and marking answers at random. We recommend that, after reading the instructions, you quickly look over the entire test to see what types of questions are included (matching, multiple choice, true-false, short answer, fill-in-the-blank, essay). If point values are assigned to the questions, be sure to budget your time accordingly. That is, you should plan to spend more time answering a question that is worth twenty-five out of 100 points than one worth ten points. Scanning the whole exam at the beginning will also reduce your chances of discovering in the last five minutes that an essay question worth thirty points is left. Always answer first the questions that you know and come back later to any that you wish to spend more time on. Allow at least five minutes at the end of the test period to check over your answers. Make sure the teachers can read your writing. If you need to cross something out, draw one heavy line through the word(s) and then write the answer you wish to be considered in the space above the cross-out. Sometimes students circle such "second" responses to be sure that the teacher knows which answer to grade.

Advice specific to objective tests.

There are several points to keep in mind when answering objective test items. The following advice refers to test questions that require you to recognize correct answers among incorrect ones (i.e., multiple choice, true-false, matching) or to recall details (fill-in-the-blanks).

1. As you read through these questions, pay special attention to all *qualifying* words such as *never, always, usually, sometimes, all, most, least, best,* or *worst.* These words provide information as to when and under what conditions a statement is or is not correct. Modifiers play their most important role in "true-false" questions.

2. When completing multiple-choice questions, first eliminate answers that are clearly incorrect. Next, review your remaining choices. How are they different? How are they alike? Does one answer address the question better than the others?

3. If you have matching questions, count to see whether the number of possible answers equals the number of words to match. Will you have to make use of some answers more than once? Will there be answers left over?

4. If you are unsure of an answer or cannot quickly reason it out, it is better to skip the question and go on to the next. You can either circle the item or put a mark (x, *, or √) next to it to identify it. If time remains at the end, then you can readily return to the unanswered questions.

5. Decide whether it's to your advantage to take "educated" guesses when you've not sure of an answer. Will you be penalized for guessing? That is, sometimes a test score is based not only on the number of questions answered correctly but also on the number answered incorrectly. If points are taken off for wrong answers, then there is a penalty for gues-

sing. In such instances, it makes more sense for you to leave the answer blank than to take a *wild* guess. On the other hand, if you're certain that some of the choices are definitely wrong and can narrow down your choices to two possible answers, the chance of getting the right answer is high. It's in your best interest to make an "educated" guess under these circumstances. If there is no added penalty for wrong answers, meaning the grade is based only on the number of correct responses, you should *not* leave any spaces blank. In this case, guessing cannot lower your score but may serve to raise your test grade.

Advice specific to subjective tests.

These tests are usually called "essay" tests and are made up of short-answer questions (paragraph response) and/or discussion questions. Essay tests measure your ability to remember what you've learned, to organize the information, to express it clearly, and to interpret and/or apply this information. When answering these types of questions, remember to:

1. Read and follow directions precisely. What are you being asked to address in your answer? Are you asked to "list, explain, discuss, compare/contrast, describe, evaluate, prove, justify, or analyze"?

2. Read the first question you plan to answer and jot down in the side margin or on scrap paper the key points or phrases you'll need to cover. Then, before you begin your response, decide how best to order these points and think about your answer for a minute or two. We suggest that you write your essay on every other line of the page. In addition to making it easier for your teacher to read your answer, it is easier for you to add information and/or to cross out and

rewrite sections of your answer without having to draw arrows directing the reader to the top or side margins.

In her book *The Report Card Trap*, Beverly Haley (Betterway Publications: 1985), a teacher for over fifteen years, stresses particular points. (1) Be sure to write in complete sentences. (2) Begin your answer with a restatement of the question. (3) Support each of your main points with a variety of specific details, important facts, examples, or explanations. Check that your points have been stated in a way that reflects clear, logical, and complete trains of thought. To this we would add, "Don't assume anything is obvious." Never assume that your teacher knows you know certain information. No matter how basic the information might be, you are better off including the information in your written answer. (4) End your response with a brief summary or concluding statement. (5) Review your answer and look for spelling, grammatical, or punctuation errors as well as for any information you may have omitted. Reread the question to be sure you've done what was asked. (6) If you are nearing the end of the testing period and realize that you will not have enough time to complete a question or questions, we recommend that you at least provide as detailed an outline as possible of your written answer. Most teachers (but not all) will give students partial credit for demonstrating some knowledge, even if a comprehensive answer has been impossible to complete.

Review all returned tests.

This is the key to "learning from your mistakes." A careful inspection of your graded exams can be valuable for at least two major reasons. First, you'll discover what information or material you haven't yet mastered. Determining where these "gaps" in knowledge or understanding lie is especially important for classes in which the material builds from one section to the next, as in math and in some science courses. You'll want to review this material again and you'll probably want to speak to your teacher if the information or concepts continue to be hard for you to grasp.

Reviewing old exams can also help you learn how to prepare better for those tests in the future. For example, can you tell whether guessing at some answers was a good idea? Should you go with your first choice of answers? Did you find that changing your answers on objective tests resulted in more right or more wrong answers? Did you budget your time appropriately? Or were there several questions you weren't able to get to at all? Did you make errors in reading the questions? Next time, read and reread questions before responding. Were you asked questions about things you didn't think were important or that weren't included in your notes? Practice asking yourself questions (see earlier study tips in this chapter), and try to make your questions similar to those your teacher asks during reviews for the next test. Pay attention in class and tune into the key ideas your teacher stresses during each lesson. This active listening is particularly important in the days just before a test, when most teachers spend some class-time reviewing material for the exam.

9

Conclusion

As we have seen, homework is important! Besides the obvious desired effect of better marks in school, good homework habits bring about later achievements in other areas of your child's life. They also bring about a much more cooperative attitude at home with you.

As you teach homework skills, you foster the important characteristics of independence and responsibility. For your child, school is analogous to an adult's job. Your child is learning how to work under supervision and to work independently. A major benefit of helping your child to develop good homework habits is helping him or her to become self-sufficient.

If you, like thousands of other parents, find that homework becomes a battleground and a struggle of wills, our program can greatly improve the atmosphere in your home and your relationship with your child. You'll replace confrontation with cooperation, and antagonism with alliance; in short, you'll win the homework war with love. If we pressure our children too much, they'll probably resist and become defiant. Just as we can "lead a horse to water but can't make him drink," so, too, we can get children into their rooms but can't get 'em to work. We can, however, work hard to develop a cooperative attitude, which motivates them to develop higher standards. We accomplish this by encouragement and cooperation, *and by the application of psychological principles* to the homework situation.

But before you apply these principles, you should, as we said in Chapter 2, determine whether there are physical or academic problems that interfere with your child's school performance. Are there vision, hearing or learning disabilities? To rule out problems in these areas, you may need professional consultation with school counselors and specialists. After that, you must attempt to win the homework war with love. You work on forming an alliance with your youngster in which both of you are cooperating toward a common goal—developing better homework habits. We develop the habits through the major guiding psychological principles of our program, which are *association* and *reinforcement*.

Association and Reinforcement

When we use association, we repeatedly match specific stimuli with specific behaviors; in other words, we form habits. Therefore, your child should learn to write down assignments in a specific place, such as an assignment book or a notebook, each time homework is given. With repetition, the habits become automatic. In the beginning, your encouragement will be required to prompt your child, but the child's habits will form with time.

The next step is to work out a homework schedule with your youngster that sets up a time and place for homework completion. Once determined, the schedule should be followed in a consistent manner. Morris, for example, develops the habit of doing homework at 3:15 P.M. every day, and soon he just does it. You should select a location that is comfortable, well lit, and as free from distractions as possible. The location should be designated the "homework spot," and only homework should be done there. Eventually, the conscious decision to do homework at the same time and same place each day becomes an automatic response, and a good homework routine has been born. We then use the principle of reinforcement to encourage timely completion of homework. Activities that your child enjoys can be used as a reinforcement. Therefore, when your child completes the homework in an acceptable manner, he or she may play, watch television, or do other enjoyable activities.

You must present the program to your child with a spirit of encouragement. Usually parental attention is the most powerful reinforcer for children, so your attention should be arranged to be dependent upon positive accomplishments. You should reinforce progress by the use of positive attention. You should minimize criticism and maximize encouragement. Praise your child for trying and doing better; don't just praise perfection. So when Morris, predictably, dawdles in the beginning, his parents must resist paying attention to the dawdling. They should encourage Morris and praise him for doing better. "Morris, it is so much better now that we don't have to argue about when you will do your homework. You are doing it at 3:15 P.M. so much better now." Remember, if attention is reinforcing, then paying attention to negative homework behaviors will inadvertently reinforce the very behaviors you wish to change. In addition, criticism often stimulates children's resistance. The rule is for the parents to *play to strength*. That is, focus on what your child is doing right, not wrong, when it comes to homework.

The principle of association is next applied as you develop a place where homework is done. If the place is a desk in Morris's bedroom, then the rule is that homework—and nothing but homework—is done at that desk, and only at that desk. This is to ensure that the association of that desk with completing homework is not watered down by associations with other activities performed at that desk. So, for example, your child must not doodle and daydream at the homework desk. The child can get up when his or her attention wanes, and doodle or daydream, but is *not* to perform these nonhomework activities at the desk. Once again, reinforcement is the prime vehicle for achieving this habit of completing only homework at just one place. In the beginning the child should be given a great deal of encouragement and praise for being at the desk. *Play to strength.*

We have developed a homework poster to be placed over the student's desk. It serves as a reminder of the procedures necessary for the development of better homework habits.

Homework Rules

1   I'LL BEGIN HOMEWORK AT _____ EVERY DAY

2   I'LL DO HOMEWORK *ONLY* AT (DESK)

3   I'LL *ONLY* DO HOMEWORK AT DESK (daydream, doodle, etc. some other place)

4   I'LL WATCH T.V., PLAY, CALL FRIENDS, ETC. *ONLY* AFTER HOMEWORK IS COMPLETED

5   I'LL TRY HARD TO DO HOMEWORK WELL—IT'S MORE FUN!

The last rule is especially important. Often, youngsters view homework as an unpleasant chore that they must get done if they don't want to get into trouble. These youngsters usually do not take pride in their homework performance. As a result, homework becomes a chore that they dread. If a youngster played basketball without being involved and just did an indifferent job, then basketball would also become a chore. It is only when we have worked hard to do a good job that we enjoy it. Basketball, like most activities, is more fun when we get involved and try hard. Even if we win, it is usually not fun unless we try hard. Youngsters do better in homework when they get involved in it and try to do it well. While homework will probably never become the child's favorite thing to do, trying hard will make it more fun.

Case Histories

To illustrate the principles that we have discussed throughout this book, we offer case histories of two children with whom we have worked. The first case involves Mario, a seventh-grader who frustrated his teachers and infuriated his parents. Mario was described by the school as "drifting out," or not paying attention in the class. His grades hovered on either side of passing. His teachers were upset because he did not seem to care about school. He rarely got into trouble for behavior, but he spent too much time daydreaming in class. Despite warnings and punishments from teachers (detention, extra homework), Mario did somewhat less than the minimum work. Often he would lie, saying that he did not have homework, and when caught he didn't seem to mind very much.

Mario's parents were fed up with him. He had an older brother and older sister who both did well in school. His parents had no idea why he was not doing his work. Their level of irritation with him spread to other areas. They simply could not talk to him amiably. When he was sent to his room to do homework, he generally started, but rarely completed the work. His parents tried a number of ways of punishing him, but to no avail. They yelled and cursed—no results; they took away privileges like television—no results; they made deals with him that they would buy him a special bicycle if he improved his grades. That incentive seemed to work well for almost a week, but then he reverted to his usual pattern of drifting out.

Mario never told his parents that they were wrong nor did he openly defy them; but his behavior still exhibited a noncompliance with homework. The school now threatened not to promote Mario unless he did homework and showed substantial improvement. The family was then advised by their pediatrician to see a psychologist.

Once contacted, we checked his school records for any indication of academic difficulty. Past testing by the school psychologist indicated that the boy was functioning in the high-average range of intelligence. There were no signs of visual or hearing problems. He had been getting satisfactory grades in school until the fifth grade, when his performance slowly started to deteriorate. No one had any idea why, and there was no specific incident that indicated that he had become angry, anxious, or not motivated in school. He just slowly started doing less and less work.

When we discussed the issue with Mario, he said that he did not want to do poorly in school. He just said that he couldn't pay attention and that sometimes school was boring. Yet, when we discussed his subjects, he showed interest in them. He liked talking about the solar system, which he was learning about in science, and he liked talking about social studies. When we asked him what the results of his doing poorly in school were, he said that it got the teachers mad at him. He denied wanting to get the teachers mad. He also replied that his parents were very mad at him for not doing his homework. He did not like it when they screamed at him and punished him. In short, he wanted to do better.

Once we heard that he was motivated to do better (as the very large majority of youngsters are), we began with the same homework rules that we presented earlier. He agreed to begin his work after supper and to do homework, and only homework, at his desk. His parents said they wanted to help Mario and not to get angry at him. We discussed how they could help with Mario and his family, and Mario felt that gentle reminders about when homework should begin and when projects were due would help. He specifically asked his parents not to nag him. He said that he disliked hearing nagging and yelling. His parents agreed not to punish him by yelling and withholding privileges. It was important for his parents to be perceived as helping. In fact, we felt that Mario's reluctance to do homework had become an attempt on his part to get his parents angry. He was angered and hurt by their criticism, and retaliated by passively avoiding homework. Their anger, then, had become reinforcing to his passive retaliation.

Although Mario's parents reported that it was difficult not to get mad at him when he forgot his homework assignment the first day, they bit their tongues and did not show their irritation. When he called a friend and got the assignment, his parents praised him for getting the information so quickly and without grumbling. He started his homework slightly later than he had agreed to, but with minimal parental nagging. Instead, they praised his efforts. He reported that he did not need to get up and take breaks as he had anticipated, and that the homework wasn't so difficult after all.

Both Mario and his parents reported an immediate improvement in his completion of homework. Mario had an exam on which he did poorly, and his parents were still concerned about his being left back. We then went over the approach to studying for exams. Mario just did not use sufficient active repetitions when preparing for tests. We drilled material with him, and his older brother agreed to help him study. Some of his math was different from the way his parents had learned it, and the brother was more helpful than they. Mario's test results improved significantly after these studying strategies were applied.

Things were apparently going very well when the report card came. We were all surprised to read that almost all his teachers reported that he was not doing his all homework. This was the opposite of what he had told us and his parents. Although none of us said so, we thought the wool might have been pulled over our eyes. Mario's parents were upset and felt that we had accomplished nothing. Mario insisted that he did indeed do his homework, something his parents had heard more than once in the past.

We then asked for a conference with his teachers. Three out of four of his teachers attended, and the other left a note saying that he had been doing adequately. The first teacher said that we had a kid who simply did not care about homework and school and we were just knocking our heads against the wall in our efforts to motivate Mario. The other teachers said that Mario's test grades had improved but that he still missed many homework assignments. When we said that we would like to know more specifics because the boy seemed very sincere when he claimed that assignments were completed, the teachers looked at their record books. Each of them then reported that he had *not* missed a single homework assignment since he had started our homework program four weeks earlier.

What had happened was that because of the long history of what seemed like indifference on Mario's part, he had developed a reputation as an apathetic student. Reputations sometimes have the effect of obscuring reality. So despite a clear improvement in school performance, the label of "poor student" hid the change in his habits.

As the meeting with the teachers went on, they began to note even more improvement. In general, they reported that Mario daydreamed less in class and participated more often. They also reported that his overall mood seemed somewhat better. Although some said that he still daydreamed and that he was not the star of their classes, there was improvement reported in each class. The improvement apparently continued, because at the end of the term, Mario and his parents were thrilled that he had passed every subject and had mainly Bs.

The second case seemed more difficult because of the intensity of the conflict. Joe's parents were divorced, and Joe's mother was having the dickens of a time placing any sort of controls on eight-year-old Joe. They would engage in big arguments whenever Joe's mother requested anything. Often the arguments became physical, with Joe hitting his mother and her retaliating. He would demand that she take him to McDonald's, and when she did, he would then insist he wanted to go to Burger King. Usually, he threw temper tantrums until he got his way.

Homework was a disaster. Whenever Joe's mother tried to get him to do homework, he simply refused. This led to real homework wars, both of them screaming and sometimes hitting. Her level of punishment increased as she felt that she had less and less control over him. She made him stay in his room some evenings, took away his toys, withheld television, and even threatened to tear up his beloved Garbage Pail Kid cards. When he attacked her, she ripped one of them. In a real sense, they were at war.

Curiously, Joe did not have any discipline problems in school. He was admonished for not doing his homework, but when detention or recess was used to have him do homework, he complied. He got along well with the other children, and was able to keep up with the schoolwork. The teacher felt that Joe could be an excellent student if he did his homework at home.

Because of Joe's level of school performance, there was no reason to suspect perceptual or learning difficulties. We concentrated on behavior. An analysis of the behavior indicated that Joe and his mother were at war. Joe's mother was frustrated and angry that she had little control over him, and she resorted to punishment as the method of gaining control. This, in turn, made Joe angry. He then retaliated in different ways. He yelled, screamed, hit, and was defiant. His goal was to upset his mother. He succeeded, and was, therefore, reinforced whenever she became angry and upset.

She, being angry at his response, also retaliated. Her goal was to control him, and she used any means

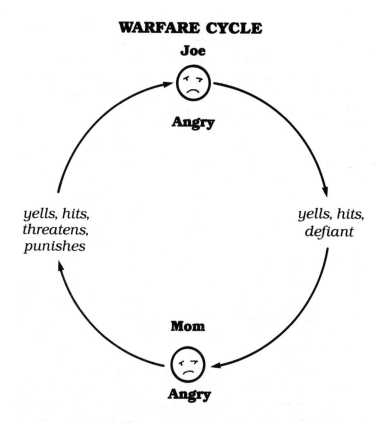

WARFARE CYCLE

Joe

Angry

*yells, hits,
threatens,
punishes*

*yells, hits,
defiant*

Mom

Angry

Illustration of Warfare in the Family

that might achieve control. Therefore, she made threats and gestures that were exaggerated and destructive: "You won't watch T.V. for a month unless you do your homework!"; or, "I'll rip up your Garbage Pail Kids unless you do homework!" These threats only made Joe angrier and more defiant. Therefore, the warfare cycle escalated. Each was reinforced by the anger of the other.

We replaced the warfare cycle with a cooperation cycle. We drew the figure that was presented and asked both of them if they liked getting angry. Both said that they hated it. Joe hated his mother's yelling, and she hated Joe's. We pointed out that every time either of them got angry, it had the effect of making the other one even angrier. Once this was pointed out to them, it became crystal clear.

We now replaced the warfare cycle with a cooperation cycle. Both agreed to a schedule of homework, a place of homework, and a standard of homework performance. Joe's mother agreed to work on not yelling so much, although she said there would be times that she failed. Joe said that he would work on not yelling, although he also said there would be mistakes. We asked them to reinforce each other with praise when improvement was noted. Joe would tell his mother that he appreciated her not yelling so much, and she would frequently tell him how much better it was for both of them when he cooperated.

They both relaxed considerably after just a few days. At the next session, they both reported significant improvement. Homework was completed every day that week. Although there were still incidents, a marked improvement was shown in their relationship. The warfare cycle had been substantially replaced. As we phased therapy out, we also worked on teaching both of them to do the "wet noodle"; that is, to relax and make their bodies as limp as a wet noodle whenever they started getting angry. This helped them avoid escalating tensions.

Although Joe's case was more dramatic than Mario's, it was no more difficult to correct. The same homework rules were applied after the homework war was won with love. Joe improved rapidly, and he and his mother were greatly relieved.

Charting Progress

We do want to have an objective method of evaluating a program's effectiveness. In order for you to determine the effectiveness of the program, we recommend that you fill in the Homework Problem Checklist weekly for the first two weeks and monthly thereafter. Try to go through the checklist independently without looking at previous results. This can help you determine changes that may not be obvious otherwise. Just as we cannot see our own children grow taller because we are too close, we often miss seeing small changes in daily homework routines. We have heard some parents mention little improvement when, in fact, there were significant changes. There is also the possibility that this program will not work for your child. You certainly would need to know this, too; answering the checklist will help you to do that.

"Mr. Osborne, may I be excused? My brain is full."

The Far Side. © 1986 by Universal Press Syndicate. Reprinted with permission. All rights reserved.

When More Help is Needed

Our research indicates that approximately 90 percent of children improved on the program; however, we are also aware that some children need more help than this program gives. If there is no change after two weeks, there are questions you should ask. Have you failed to give frequent encouragement? Have you been critical, even in a subtle way (such as tone of voice)? Have you been consistent? Parents should try to ask themselves, and each other, whether they are critical or supportive. If they have been supportive, we should review the other principles about time and place. Are they being tried *consistently*? Consistency, contrary to Ralph Waldo Emerson, is not the hobgoblin of little minds. Consistency is necessary for the development of habits. Consistency is especially important when habits are to be ignored. If attention is periodically paid to poor habits, the attention may intermittently reinforce those habits. Parents should review their own behavior to determine whether they are applying the program consistently.

One approach recommended by some psychologists that we do *not* recommend except under professional supervision is the use of backup reinforcers. For example, parents frequently tell their children that they will give them a bike if they do better in school. By and large, this does not work, and when it does, there may be undesirable side effects. We once gave our four-year-old son a matchbox car for voluntarily keeping his room tidy. Later in the day, when he was asked to give us a hug, he replied that he would for a reward. By giving rewards, we sometimes teach the child to work for the reward and not for the activity.

Therefore, if the reward is removed, the child will stop engaging in the activity. Levine and Fasbacht wrote about this and claimed that giving token rewards may lead to token learning. In almost all cases, the rewards of getting recognition, decreasing tension, and doing a good job are more than sufficient to encourage homework improvements.

Still, in some cases professional help may be needed. We have found that those families that require more help usually have more intense emotional problems that interfere with other areas of living. Also, there are some adolescents who just find school, at this time, irrelevant to their future goals. One such teenager wanted to be a rock guitarist. Although we had him in the school band, he spent all his time practicing his instrument, which was more important to him than school. Other specific problems that may interfere are social problems in school; for example, the youngster who is victimized by peers. Once again, we caution that learning disabilities and/or perceptual problems should be evaluated, as they can lead to the homework task being more difficult for the child. Professional help can be useful in determining the individual problems that are keeping the child and parent from developing an alliance that will help with school. To repeat, our evidence indicates that the overwhelming number of parents will benefit from our program.

Final Word

Homework is very important, but it is just one aspect of the child's life. We have two goals in raising children, and we feel that these goals should be incorporated into all aspects of our children's lives. Those two goals are that children should grow up to be self-sufficient as well as comfortable with themselves. If homework becomes an area of life with too much parental involvement, it may deprive your youngster of learning to be independent. Be judicious when deciding how much help your child needs. Beware of the feeling that you, and not your child, are being graded in school. When you become unnecessarily anxious about adequate school performance, you may do more for your child than necessary and prevent the development of self-reliance. Parents can do too much for children. We all want our children to grow, but if we feed them too much they simply become overweight. In the same light, there are times that we psychologists have recommended that parents withdraw from the homework contest because they are doing too much. In rare, special cases, we have even allowed some teenage children to fail courses rather than have the parent essentially pass the course for the child. In those cases, we felt it was more important that the child learn self-sufficiency rather than that "Mom will take care of it." Because of the premium we place on teaching self-sufficiency to children, we advocate that parents always look to shaping the child's homework activities toward independent completion. Younger children, of course, require more support than older children. But in all cases, phasing out of parental activities is the goal.

It is also important to realize that parental anxiety over homework can interfere with the youngster growing up at ease with him or herself. If homework and schoolwork are overemphasized and demands made on the child are not congruent with the child's abilities and temperament, the child may feel that he or she is a failure. There are many cases where the parental expectations for children are unrealistic. Interestingly, we see this most often in children with high levels of achievement rather than low. These children may be getting nearly all As in coursework, with one B. Some parents then begin to express disapproval of the B. In some children the disapproval is motivating, but in others the B may represent the best the youngster can do. Some children may be good at science but not at English. If the child is attempting the work with integrity, then the parents should be comfortable with the B. We advocate emphasizing effort rather than performance.

Kids, being people, differ from each other. Not all can be academic stars. Just as some children are better at basketball than others, some children are better at schoolwork than others. The standard that you expect should be based on a complete picture of your child's abilities and interests, not on some abstract standard of performance. We must respect children for being themselves, individuals. Your child must not feel doomed to failure because he or she can't possibly meet your standards, no matter how hard he or she tries. If your standard is unrealistically high, it may well make the child anxious, and may actually interfere with school performance. Some children simply turn away from school because they feel that whatever they do is not good enough. By emphasizing effort rather than achievement, we reduce this risk.

Winning the homework war with love can be a positive experience for you and your child. The program we have presented has worked with many parents, and we think that you can do it, too. It will take change on your part in the beginning, but it is well worth the effort. We think that it can significantly improve your child's homework habits. But more important, we think that our program can lead to a home life in which the homework war is replaced with cooperation. Other parents have done it. So can you!

Homework Program Evaluation

Please take a few moments to answer the following questions about your experiences in reading this book and applying the methods described in it when working with your child. Your feedback will provide us with information about how effective this homework program has been for you and your child. Your responses to the following questions will enable us to improve the program in the future. Thanks for your help!

Your child's age: _____   Your child's sex: _____

Your child's grade in school: _____

1. When you *first* completed the Homework Problem Checklist on page 47 for your child before starting the program, she/he received a total score of _____ (fill in score).

2. The three major homework problems you and your child have been having are:

   a. _____

   _____

   ======

191

b._____

_____

c._____

_____

3. How helpful has the book been for you? (Circle the number that best represents your answer)

1	2	3	4	5	6	7
Not at all	Very little	Little		Somewhat helpful	Helpful	Very helpful

4. How understandable was the material covered in the book?

1	2	3	4	5	6	7
Not at all	Very difficult to understand	Difficult		Somewhat understand- able	Under- standable	Very easy to understand

5. What chapters and/or homework suggestions in the book were the most helpful?

6. Which homework exercises in the book were the *most* helpful?

7. What chapters and/or suggestions in the book were the *least* helpful? If possible, tell us why you felt this way.

8. Which homework exercises were the *least* helpful? Why do you think this was so?

9. Were there homework problem areas that were not covered in the book that should be included? What would these be?

10. To what extent did this book meet your expectations?

1	2	3	4	5	6	7
Did not meet expectations at all						Very much met my expectations

11. How confident would you be in recommending this book to a friend who was having similar problems with his/her child?

1	2	3	4	5	6	7
Not all all confident						Very confident

12. If you completed the Homework Problem Checklist a second time after trying out one or more suggestions included in this book, what score did your child receive this time? _____
(fill in score here)

OTHER COMMENTS:

Please return this questionnaire to:

Dr. Kathleen Anesko & Fredric M. Levine
c/o Barbara Gilson—Reference Division
MONARCH PRESS
Gulf & Western Building, 16th Floor
1 Gulf & Western Plaza
New York, NY 10023

Research Findings of the Homework Clinic

Nearly fifty families with children in elementary school participated in a study we did to evaluate how effective a parent manual entitled *Homework Hassles: How to Handle Them* was in reducing the number of homework problems commonly encountered by parent and child. All children attended regular classrooms, but more than one-third were receiving remedial-education services in the form of resource-room help or tutoring. Half of the families were given the manual to use at home on their own, while the other half met in small groups once a week with their professional trainers to review the suggestions described in the booklet.

After one month, parents in both programs reported significant decreases in homework difficulties. Scores on the Homework Problem Checklist dropped an average of 10 to 12 points for both groups. Furthermore, according to daily homework ratings made by the parents, children in both groups were completing homework without incident, in a reasonable amount of time, and with less help from their parents on four out of every five days that homework was assigned. Many of the children, too, noted changes in their parents' behavior; they reported that Mom or Dad were "being nice, not yelling, and being more understanding when I make a mistake." At the conclusion of the one-month program, they routinely assigned grades of either A or B to the quality of homework supervision their parents provided. According to their program evaluation ratings, parents were equally satisfied with their training program, whether they attended group meetings led by a mental health professional or worked at home, alone, with the manual.

These research results, which strongly suggest that parents successfully apply written strategies for managing their children's homework problems without professional guidance, also provide the rationale for writing this book. What follows are a series of "case sketches" that describe the experiences of six families who completed the "self-help" homework program.

Homework Program Case Studies

The Roberts Family

Paul was an eight-year-old third-grader whose mother sought help when the classroom teacher informed her that he might not be promoted to the fourth grade because of poor academic performance. He was described as easily distracted, silly, and restless, and although he did well on achievement tests, was completing homework on only one or two days out of every five that it was assigned. At the time that Mrs. Roberts began to use the programs outlined in this book,

Paul's score on the Homework Problem Checklist was 36, indicating *serious* homework problems.

Mrs. Roberts decided to work first on the problem of Paul's difficulty in concentrating on his homework assignments. At the start of the program, Paul was required to sit at the kitchen table while his mother went about her household chores. Paul's eight-month-old sister sat in a playpen near the table where he was working so that Paul could keep an eye on her while his mother prepared dinner. As Mrs. Roberts surveyed Paul's usual homework scene, she quickly became aware of how many distractions were present that interfered with Paul's ability to focus on his work. It came as no surprise when she observed him out of his seat an average of fifteen times during each hour of "homework time." She noted that he spent most of this out-of-seat time playing with his sister, who giggled and cooed in response to his funny faces and nursery rhyme songs. When he wasn't entertaining his sister, Paul would usually call out for his mother to come and help him with his work.

Mother and son then worked out a schedule for homework that included a regular time and place for its completion. They decided that Paul would start homework at 4:00 P.M., having had an hour to play with his friends or with his sister to use up some of his excess energy. During that hour of play, Mrs. Roberts would feed the baby and get her ready for a late-afternoon nap, removing one major distraction for Paul. At 4:00, Paul would go to his room, sit at his desk (which had been cleared of his baseball cards and wrestling magazines), and start his work. His mother made sure that she popped in every fifteen minutes to praise Paul's progress in completing his assignments and to answer questions he might have about the work, thus reducing the number of times he got out of his seat and got involved in nonhomework activities. As he became able to complete larger portions of his assignments without first asking for help, she planned to lengthen gradually the intervals between her visits to Paul's room and to praise his growing ability to work independently.

How successful was the program? When we met with Mrs. Roberts and Paul six weeks after they had set up and since stuck to a homework routine, Paul's score on the Homework Problem Checklist had dropped to 19. Some problems still existed—there were days when Paul came out of his room three or four times during his homework hour—but mother and son were able to focus on Paul's improvement and were confident that things could only get better when it came to homework.

The Cohen Family

Sarah, a lively nine-year-old in the fourth grade, and her mother had been struggling with homework since the girl entered third grade, about the time Sarah's parents had separated. The youngster's score of 22 on the Homework Problem Checklist indicated serious problems; Sarah always put off the starting of homework, was easily distracted once she began the work, and hurried through her work so that she often made mistakes or produced papers that were hard to read. Sarah's mother, Ms. Cohen, after a ten-hour day at the store she owned and managed, often lost her temper and snapped at Sarah while supervising her homework. Ms. Cohen realized that she would have to change her own way of relating to Sarah over homework in order for Sarah's performance to improve. For every compliment or encouragement given to Sarah, Ms. Cohen made four to five critical remarks—an uncomfortable situation for mother as well as for daughter.

Like Mrs. Roberts, Ms. Cohen decided that homework should be completed in the child's room to cut down on distractions. Furthermore, she and Sarah agreed that homework would be started somewhat later in the afternoon, around 5:30 P.M., half an hour after Ms. Cohen returned from work and had a chance to relax. As a result, Ms. Cohen approached her role of homework supervisor in a more positive frame of mind, and found that, under these circumstances, she had little difficulty identifying things to praise in her daughter's work.

Even so, Sarah continued to struggle with schoolwork, and her next report-card marks did not reflect the hours she and her mother had devoted to homework completion. Ms. Cohen requested that her daughter be tested by the school psychologist, since she had read that learning disabilities sometimes do not become evident until the child reaches third or fourth grade, when the demands of school increase.

The test results indicated that, while Sarah was a child of average-to-bright-average intelligence, she was experiencing severe enough difficulties with reading and language arts skills to be classified "reading disabled" or "dyslexic." In order to master the ability to read and understand her schoolbooks, Sarah would require different instruction and learning materials from those she was receiving in her classroom. Ms. Cohen, Sarah's teacher, and the school psychologist all agreed that Sarah could benefit from placement in a smaller classroom with a teacher who had specialized training in learning disabilities. It was thought that once schoolwork was adjusted to meet Sarah's special learning needs, she would experience less frustration and subsequently struggle less with homework. Recognition of Sarah's *real* learning problems also enabled Ms. Cohen to redefine their past conflict over homework as her daughter's reduced ability to learn when taught by standard classroom methods, rather than as acts of defiance directed at Mom or as indifference toward learning in general.

The Walters Family

Soon after Mrs. Walters met with us to discuss her eight-year-old son's homework problems, she called to tell us that Todd had been diagnosed as having an "attention-deficit disorder." The family doctor was going to try him on a low dosage of Ritalin, a drug that has been shown to increase some children's ability to concentrate. She was hopeful that the medication would make him less distractible during homework time and thus cut down on the time she had to "stay on top of him" while the homework was getting done.

Since Todd's Homework Problem Checklist score of 38 reflected a variety of difficulties beyond distractibility, we encouraged Mrs. Walters to read through the manual and apply those suggestions that might help mother and son deal with Todd's tendency to rush through his work, make numerous mistakes, and produce messy papers, even with his mother in the room. Mrs. Walters was also concerned that Todd often denied having homework when, in fact, assignments had been given, a behavior she referred to as "deliberate lying."

It was clear that Mrs. Walters was very emotionally involved in her son's homework performance, to the point where she had become "part of the problem." When reading the section of the manual that discussed parent attitudes about homework, she found herself remembering back to her experiences as a young schoolchild. She recalled how her parents had sat beside her, insisting that her papers be neatly completed and that all answers be correct, even if that meant she had to spend hours each night at her desk. Mrs. Walters also remembered how angry she sometimes felt toward her parents and how ashamed, too, when, despite long hours of studying, she came home with lower grades on tests than she usually got. Now, here she was, twenty years later, doing the same thing to her son!

After talking with Todd's teacher, Mrs. Walters found out that her expectations for her son's homework performance were higher than what could be reasonably expected of a child his age with a known attention-deficit disorder. While she worked on adjusting her expectations, Mrs. Walters decided to ask the high-school student who babysat when she was working to supervise Todd's homework during the week. Within two weeks, homework time was calmer and Todd would proudly show his mother what he'd accomplished when she arrived home from the office. Mrs. Walters would check over his assignments, at times *suggest* a few corrections, and praise the effort her son had put into the work. She also learned to grit her teeth and let some papers go into school with erasure marks, a couple of misspelled words, or a mathematical error or two. Todd's teacher would provide the necessary feedback, not her.

Interestingly enough, one month after Mrs. Walters put this program into effect, she observed that nearly all homework assignments arrived home; homework was "forgotten" only once in ten days, as compared to six times in ten days beforehand. His Homework Problem Checklist score dropped 17 points to 29, a score that continued to reflect problems with distractibility and concentration but that also represented reduced frustration with the work and with his own performance.

The Burkart Family

Sometimes parents identify so many problems when it comes to getting homework done, they just don't know where to begin. Such was the case with Mrs. Burkart, whose eight-and-a-half-year-old daughter, Melanie, scored a 36 on the Homework Problem Checklist when they were first seen! This friendly, good-natured third-grader was reported to have almost daily problems in the following areas: bringing all necessary books and papers home, complaining about the work, and becoming easily frustrated to the point where she would criticize her own work. Melanie was described as highly distractible; she had to be reminded several times to start her assignments, and because of her procrastination and daydreaming, took up to three hours to complete her work. Her teacher indicated that *when* the homework was completed, it was generally well done. However, assignments were often late or missing, much to the dismay of the mother and teacher. Melanie was also expected to bring home any classwork that wasn't finished, so sometimes she had twice the homework that her classmates had.

Mrs. Burkart decided that the first problem to tackle was how to make sure that Melanie brought home all the books, dittos, workbooks, and assignments needed to complete daily homework. She and Melanie went shopping and picked out a folder and small notebook that had the girl's favorite cartoon characters on the covers. Dittos and assignment sheets were to be kept in the folder, and completed homework papers were to be returned to the teacher. All assignments that were written on the board were to be copied into the notebook. It was hoped that these organizational aids would help Melanie keep track of what she was supposed to take home each night.

During the first few weeks, Melanie's teacher agreed to check over Melanie's folder and notebook to be sure that every assignment was recorded and that all papers needed for the night's work were in the folder. He also checked that incomplete classwork was placed in the folder. Praise was given when all papers and assignments were in order, and a brief note indicating Melanie's success was written in the notebook for Mrs. Burkart to see. Each day that Melanie came home with all homework materials, she earned an extra thirty minutes of play time.

How well did this program work? We had Mrs. Burkart keep track of how many days each week Melanie came home with missing homework books and materials. The week before the Burkarts started the program, Melanie failed to bring home one or more schoolbooks four days out of five; she also had to call classmates on three out of five nights because she hadn't copied down all assignment information while in class. After one month of using the folder/notebook system, Melanie was bringing home everything she needed for homework at least three or four days each week. Not perfect, but better! Now mother and daughter are working to reduce the number of reminders that are given before Melanie begins her homework, as well as the amount of time it takes her to do the work once she starts. Mrs. Burkart plans to meet with Melanie's teacher to determine why Melanie is having trouble finishing her work in school. She also wants to figure out how to help her daughter to concentrate better on classwork so that she doesn't have hours of homework each evening. Good parent-teacher communication is paying off for everyone involved.

The Gruen Family

Mrs. Gruen was unprepared for the problems her son Dean, a third-grader, presented when it came to homework. Her oldest child, a nine-year-old daughter, was self-motivated and completed all her work without prompting or reminders. Dean, on the other hand, was easily distracted, quickly became frustrated with the work, and demanded much assistance from his mother, yet responded poorly to her feedback when told to correct his work.

As suggested in this book, Mrs. Gruen sat down with Dean to talk about what was making homework time so difficult, and also observed their interactions during homework sessions for about a week. She discovered several things: Dean's five-year-old brother would move in and out of the dining room while Dean worked. More often than not, he'd try to get his older brother's attention by making animal noises, grabbing at his brother's books, or playing near the table with his motorized toys. The youngster's efforts usually paid off, as Dean would yell at him, call for "Mom," or join his brother on the floor.

Mr. and Mrs. Gruen had Dean choose a desk at a nearby store that was then put in his bedroom. This desk became the "official" homework desk, and the bedroom was made "off limits" to the younger brother while Dean was studying. They also taught Dean how to ignore his brother's "nudgy" behaviors on those occasions when the youngster slipped past Mom or Dad's watchful eyes. Even so, Mrs. Gruen found herself in Dean's room for more than half of the ninety minutes that it usually took Dean to finish his work. She felt that he wouldn't keep working unless prompted; instead, he would just sit and stare at the assignment sheet or at the page in his textbook. He just didn't seem to know how to start the work unless she went over the directions with him.

At that point, Mrs. Gruen decided to teach Dean how to use self-instruction in figuring out what steps he had to take in order to solve a problem or to answer a question. As described in this book, she first modeled how to ask and answer questions about the assignment before encouraging Dean to give the answers. She then praised him for stating each step he would take in completing the problem or question. She also had him compare his performance on earlier parts of an assignment with his current work when she wanted to direct his attention to differences in neatness or accuracy. Gradually, Dean began to "talk himself through" his assignments with only occasional supervision by his mother (for example, she'd stop by his room once every thirty minutes). Understandably, more help was given when Dean was assigned work covering new concepts, such as division, or when long-term projects were given, such as book reports. According to Mrs. Gruen, Dean was tackling homework with greater confidence and fewer problems, as noted by the drop in score from 24 to 13 on the Homework Problem Checklist.

The Arroyo Family

As evidenced in the earlier case studies, elementary-school children seem to experience common problems—such as limited concentration, procrastination, and rushing through the work—when it comes to getting homework done. Ileana Arroyo was no exception. This bright nine-year-old required many reminders before beginning her work, and without one of her parents or grandmother in the room, she would rush through her work, creating sloppy papers filled with careless mistakes. With this approach to homework, it wasn't surprising that Ileana's first score on the Homework Problem Checklist was a 27. Nor was it surprising that her teacher reported only partially completed assignments, and that what was turned in was for one, "fair" in terms of neatness and, on the average, only rarely more than 50 percent correct.

Mrs. Arroyo knew her daughter loved games and especially loved winning games, so she tried to figure out how she could make homework more "game-like" for Ileana and at the same time increase the quality of the child's homework product. Together, mother and daughter constructed a large clock face with movable hands that had the words "Beat the Clock" printed in large letters at the base. The idea of the game was to have Ileana guess how long it would take her to complete her homework that day. The clock hands would then be set for the time she had predicted. After homework was done, Ileana would check the kitchen clock and figure out whether she had finished over or under the time.

Mrs. Arroyo used the method detailed in this book for setting homework goals that increase in difficulty as the child's performance improves. That is, first she and her daughter agreed that Ileana would "win" the game when she finished the work within the predicted amount of time to or less *and* made no more than, say, ten errors. The actual number of errors allowed depended on the type of assignment she had to complete. Since math was Ileana's hardest subject, more errors were initially permitted on those assignments than were allowed for spelling, language, or social studies. As the accuracy of Ileana's work improved, fewer and fewer mistakes were acceptable in order to win the "Beat the Clock" game.

Mrs. Arroyo also tied in the use of natural consequences to the game by stating that Ileana's weekly visit to Friendly's for ice cream would be the bonus for "beating the clock" at least three days out of every five. Again, as Ileana's performance improved, the "price" of this special visit went up to five days in a row each week of timely, accurate homework completion. It should come as no surprise that Ileana's last Homework Problem Checklist score was in the average range!

Now it is up to you to try!

Bibliography

Anesko, K.M. (1986). *A comparison of minimal-contact bibliotherapy and brief parent training for the management of children's homework problems.* Unpublished doctoral dissertation, State University of New York, Stony Brook, N.Y.

Anesko, K.M., Levine, F.M., O'Leary, S.G., Shoiock, G. (1983). *Homework hassles: How to handle them* (rev. ed.). Unpublished manuscript, State University of New York at Stony Brook, Department of Psychology, Stony Brook, N.Y.

Anesko, K.M., Shoiock, G., Ramirez, R., Levine, F.M. (in press). *The Homework Problem Checklist: Assessing children's homework difficulties. Behavioral Assessment.*

Becker, W.C. (1971). *Parents are teachers: A child management program.* Champaign, IL.: Research Press.

Brehm, J. (1966). *A theory of psychological reactance.* New York: Academic Press.

Chandler, J., Argyris, D., Barnes, W., Goodman, I., Snow, C. (1985). Parents as teachers: Observations of low-income parents and children in a homework-like task. In B. Schieffelin & P. Gilmore (Eds.), *Ethnographic studies of literacy.* Norwood, N.J.: Ablex Press.

Cohn, M. (1979). *Helping your teen-age student.* New York: E.P. Dutton.

Gallup, A.M. (1985). The 17th annual Gallup poll of public's attitudes toward the public schools. *Phi Delta Kappan, 67,* 35-47.

Gallup, G.H. (1984). The 16th annual Gallup poll of public's attitudes toward the public schools. *Phi Delta Kappan, 66,* 23-38.

207

Haley, B. (1985). *The report card trap.* White Hall, VA.: Betterway Publications.

James, W. (1983). *The principles of psychology: A brief course.* Cambridge, MA.: Harvard University Press.

Levine, F.M. and Fastnacht, G. (1974). Token rewards may lead to token learning. *American Psychologist, 29*(11), 816-820.

National Commission on Excellence in Education. (1983). *A nation at risk: The imperative for educational reform.* Washington, D.C.: Department of Education.

Paschal, R.A., Weinstein, T., Walberg, H.J. (1984). The effects of homework on learning: A quantitative synthesis. *Journal of Educational Research, 78,* 97-104.

Pavlov, I. (1927). *Conditioned reflexes* (trans. by G. V. Anrep). New York: Oxford University Press.

Plessen, U., Bommert, H. (1978). Entwicklung eines Fragebogens zur Erfassung von Belastungen bei Hausaufgaben von Schulern aus 3./4. Klassen [Development of a questionnaire that comprehends homework-evoked stress among third and fourth-grade schoolage children]. *Psychologie in Erziehung und Unterricht, 25,* 16-23.

Robinson, F. (1946). *Effective study.* New York: Harper & Brothers.

Roselle, D. (1981). *Our common heritage: A world history.* Lexington, MA.: Ginn and Company.

Sheff, H., Levine, F.M. (1981). *Warfare in the family: A behavioral-cognitive model of child abuse.* Unpublished manuscript, State University of New York at Stony Brook, Department of Psychology, Stony Brook, N.Y.

Skinner, B.F. (1953). *Science and human behavior.* New York: Macmillan.

Stixrud, W. (1986, April). *Stop fighting with your child over homework—Now! Network,* pp. 5-6.

Student study-guide: How students, parents, and teachers, working together, can improve student study skills. (1984). Smithtown, N.Y.: Smithtown Central School District.

Thorndike, E.L. (1911) *Animal intelligence.* New York: Macmillan.

Other Recommended Reading for Parents

Baron, B., C. Baron, MacDonald, B. (1983). *What did you learn in school today? A comprehensive guide to getting the best possible education for your child*. New York: Warner Books.

Berry, J.W. (1982). *What to do when your mom or dad says, "Do your homework (schoolwork)"*. Chicago: Childrens' Press.

Brown, M.C. (1985). *Schoolwise: A parent's guide to getting the best education for your child*. Los Angeles, CA.: Jeremy P. Tarcher, Inc.

United States Department of Education. (1986). *What works: Research about teaching and learning*. Washington, D.C.: U.S. Department of Education.

Weinstein, C.E., Wittrock, M.C., Underwood, V.L., Schulte, A.C. (1983). *How to help your children achieve in school*. Washington, D.C.: National Institute of Education.

Zifferblatt, S.M. (1970). *Improving study and homework behaviors*. Champaign, IL.: Research Press.

Index

Access, study area, 87–89
Alarm clock, latchkey
    children, 107
Anesko, K., 5–6, 46
Anger, 37, 40, 52, 56, 59, 64,
    177–179, 181–183
Anxiety, parents, 188–189
Argyris, D., 5
Assignments
    checking with teacher, 80–
        82
    checklist, 80–81
    long-term. See Long-term
        projects
    notebook, 76–79, 173–174,
        202
    writing down, 74–76
        failure to, 70–73, 85

Association, habit
    development, 31–32,
    33, 173–177
Asthma, 25
Attention, negative vs.
    positive, 37, 126–128
Attention problems, 23–26
    attention-deficit disorder,
        24, 199, 200
    medication, 24–25
Attention span, 93–94
Auditory problems, 16–19

Backpacks, 84
Barnes, W., 5
Becker, Wesley, 126
Bibliography, 147–148

Blaming vs. problem-solving,
110–112
Bommert, H., 5
Bookbags, 84
Brehm, Jack, 110

California Achievement Test,
20
Case studies, 8–9, 177–185
homework clinic, 195–206
Census Bureau, 3
Chandler, J., 5
Checklist, assignment, 80–
81; see also Homework
Problem Checklist
Cohn, Marvin, 147, 148
Complaining child, 133–135
Computers, school, 82–83
Concentration, 196, 201, 205;
see also Distractions
Consistency, 132–133, 135,
186
Cramming, 163
Criticism, 197–198
Cylert, 24

Daydreaming, 64, 92, 93, 94
Defiance, 111
Defusing war, 108–112
Dexedrine, 24
Dilantin, 25
Disorganization, 52, 83–84
Distractions, 86–87, 196, 199,
201, 203–204; see also
Concentration
DSCG (cromolyn sodium), 25
Dyscalculia, 22
Dysgraphia, 22
Dyslexia, 22–23, 198

Einstein, Albert, 76–77
Emerson, Ralph Waldo, 186
Eme, R. [n.i.], 2
Encyclopedia, 146–147
Epilepsy, 25
Europe, 2
Expectations, parents, 200
Extinction burst,
inappropriate behavior,
135
Extracurricular activities, 104

Fatigue, 91
Feedback, 121, 123, 126–127
Fidgeting, 136–137
Folders, 83–84, 202
Frustration, 25–26, 82

Gallup Polls, 4
Game, homework as, 205–
206
Gardner, Howard, 19
Getting homework home, 52–
53, 68–85
avoid criticism, 69–70, 78
avoid punishment, 70
bookbag/backpack, 84
classmates' phone
numbers, 82
computers, school, 82–83
extra set of books, 84
folders, 83–84, 202
notebook, 76–79, 173–174,
202
decorated, 76–77, 83
dedicated, 76, 77
reinforcement (praise), 78–
79, 82

relations with teacher, 69–70, 79–80
repetition, 78
Goals, 206
definition, projects, 145–146
setting, 115–120
and self-mastery, 116
skill levels, 116–118
Goldiamond,Israel, 94
Goodman, I., 5

Habit development, 10–12, 13, 27–45, 96
association, 31–32, 33
repetition, importance, 29–31
stimulus control, 32–33
see also Reinforcement
Harley, Beverly, 170
Hearing problems, 16–19
Helping Your Teenage Student, 148
Home situation, 58–60
Homework
checklist, 80–81
common problems, 7–9
as game, 205–206
research, 2–4
schedule, 174
war, defusing, 108–112
see also Assignments; Getting homework home; Homework Problem Checklist; How to do homework
Homework Clinic, 194–206
case studies, 195–206

Homework Hassles: How to Handle Them, 194
Homework Problem
Checklist, 46–67, 68, 73, 185, 191, 194, 196, 197, 199, 201, 205, 206
attacking problem, 61–64
average scores, by sex, 51
common problems, 52–57
how to do, 55, 108–143
what to do, 52–53, 68–85
when to do, 53–54, 85–107
where to do, 54, 86–107
why to do, 55–57, 59
describing/observing problem, 65–67
listed, 47–50
Homework Program
Evaluation, 191–193
How to do homework, 108–143
defusing homework war, 108–112
goal setting, 115–120
skill levels, 116–118
ignoring child, 133–137
consistency, 133, 135
whining child, 133, 134–135
incentives, natural, 128–133
long-term projects, 114–115
parental attention/encouragement, 120–128
descriptive vs. judgmental praise, 120–121
feedback, 121, 123, 126–127

positive cf. negative attention, 126–128
words, phrases, gestures, listed, 123
parents as homework consultants, 137–139
time limits, 138–139
reinforcement, 118, 122, 126, 129, 130, 135, 137
review of assignments and materials, 113, 114
schedule and time estimation, 112–115
self-instruction training, 139–143
problem-solving, 143
talk-it-out method, 139–143
Hyperactivity/attention-deficit disorders, 24, 199, 200

Incentives, natural, 128–133
Independence, 55
Index cards
Homework Assignment Checklist, 80–81
papers, 147–148
Iowa Test of Basic Skills, 20
I.Q., 18, 19–21, 23

James, William, 30–31, 34
Japan, 2

Keith, T., 3,

Latchkey children, 106–107

Learning disabilities, 13–14, 21–23, 198
above-average I.Q., 21, 23
Levine, F.M., 5
Levine, Marilyn, 153
Librarians, 146, 147, 152–153
Lighting, 91, 92
Long-term projects, 77–78, 114–115, 144–154
goal definition, 145–146
indentifying people to help, 152–154
outline development, 148–151
plan of attack, 145
procrastination, 144–145
timetable development, 151–152
topic selection, 146–148

Miller, Louise, 153
Motivation, 55, 108, 110, 120, 179

National Commission on Excellence in Education, 2–3
A Nation at Risk, 2
Negative attention, 37, 126–128
The New York Times Index, 147, 153, 154
Noise
background, 18–19
study area, 89–90
Notebook, assignment, 76–78, 79, 173–174, 202
decorated, 76–77, 83
dedicated, 76, 77

Note taking, 155–159, 161
    reviewing, 159

Objective tests, 167–169
Ocular coordination, 16; *see
    also* Visual problems
O'Leary, S.G., 46
Outline development, papers,
    148–151

Papers. *See* Long-term
    projects
Parents, 5–7
    anxiety, 188–189
    control, 111
    expectations, 200
    praise, 123, 179–180
    surveillance, 54
    see also under How to do
        homework
Parents Are Teachers, 126
Paschal, R.A., 3
Pavlov, Ivan, 31–32, 34
Phenobarbital, 25
Phonetic spelling errors,
    learning disabilities, 22
Plessen, U., 5
Praise, 78–79, 82, 179–180
    descriptive vs. judgmental,
        120–121
    words, phrases, and
        gestures listed, 123
    see also Reinforcement
Principles of Psychology
    (James), 30–31
Problem checklist. *See*
    Homework Problem
    Checklist
Problem solving, 143

vs. person-blaming, 110–
    112
Procrastination, 72–73, 85,
    144–145
Psychologist, consulting,
    186–187, 198–199
Punishment, 34–36, 38, 44,
    45, 182, 183
    avoid, 70
    dangers, 39–40
    see also Reinforcement

Ramirez, R., 5
Reactance, 110
*Reader's Guide to Periodical
    Literature*, 147, 153,
    154
Reinforcement, 34–43, 173–
    177
    and getting homework
        home, 78–79, 82
    how to do homework, 118,
        122, 126, 129, 130,
        135, 137
    increasing effectiveness of,
        38–39
    individual definition, 36–37
    intermittent, 42–43, 44
    play to strength, 173, 174
    and punishment, 34–36,
        38, 44, 45
    dangers, 39–40
    shaping, 40–42, 102, 118
Reinforcers, backup, 186–187
Repetition, habit
    development, 29–31
    getting homework home,
        78
The Report Card Trap, 170
Reputation, student, effect on

teacher's judgment,
180–181
Research, homework, 2–4
Reviewing
    assignments, 113, 114
    test preparation, 162–166
    cramming, 163
    schedule, 163–164
Ritalin, 24, 199
Robinson, Frank, 160
Rules. *See* Study rules

Schedule, study, 94–97, 104–
    105, 174
    tests, 163–164
    and time estimation, 112–
    115
Self-instruction, 139–143,
    204
    problem-solving, 143
    talk-it-out method, 139–143
Self-mastery, 116
Self-sufficiency as goal, 188
Shaping, reinforcement, 40–
    42, 102, 118
Shoiock, G., 5, 46
Skill levels, 116–118
Skinner, B.F., 36, 40
Snow, C., 5
Social butterflies, 102–106
SQ3R method, 160–162
State University of New York
    at Stony Brook, 11
Stimulus control, habit
    development, 32–33
Stixrud, William, 138–139
Study area, 86–90, 174, 175
    access, 87–89

bedroom vs. kitchen, 89–
    90, 101–102
lighting, 91, 92
noise, 89–90
study alone, 89–90
Study rules, 91–100
    attention span, 93–94
    fatigue, 91
    one study area, 91–94
    only homework in study
        area, 92–94
    posting rules, 98–100, 176
    problems with, 100–107
    schedule, 94–97, 104–105
Study strategies, tests, 159–
    160
SQ3R method, 160–162
Subjective tests, 169–170
Surveillance, parental, 54

Talk-it-out method, 139–143
Teachers
    authority, 109
    avoid criticism of, 69–70,
        78
    relationships with, 10–11,
        69–70, 79–80, 180–
        181
    talking with, 57–58
Telephone
    calls, latchkey children,
        106–107
    numbers, classmates, 82
Test preparation, 154–166
    classroom, 155
    note taking, 155–159, 161
    reviewing, 159
    reviewing for test, 162–166
    cramming, 163

schedule, 163–164
study strategies, 159–160
   SQ3R method, 160–162
   underlining, 161–162
Test taking, 154, 166–171
   guesses, educated, 168–169
   objective tests, 167–169
   questions
      qualifiers, 168
      skipping, 168
   read directions, 166–167
   reviewing returned tests,
      170–171
   subjective tests, 169–170
   using time wisely, 167
Theophylline, 25
Thorndike, Edward, 35
Time estimation, 112–115

Time limits, 138–139
Timetable, 151–152
Topic selection, papers/
   projects, 146–148

Underlining books, test
   preparation, 161–162
University of Illinois, 6

Visual problems, 14–16

Walberg, H.J., 3
Warfare cycle, 183–184
   cf. cooperation cycle, 184
Weinstein, T., 3
Whining child, 133–135

About the Authors

Dr. Fredric M. Levine is Associate Professor of Psychology, State University of New York at Stony Brook. He has published many articles and contributed to several books.

Dr. Kathleen M. Anesko is the Coordinator of Project Natural Setting Therapeutic Management, Division of Psychological Services, Fairleigh Dickinson University. She conducted the Homework Clinic and published a research paper on the subject while at SUNY Stony Brook.